75 Tips for Internet Marketing

Contents

75 Tips for Internet Marketing 1
   Google Adsense 5
      3 Reasons Why Adsense Is Essential For Content Sites 6
      5 Ways To Improve Your Adsense Earnings 8
      Don't Get Caught With Google Adsense Click Fraud 10
      Google Adsense - The Easiest Money To Make Online? 12
      How To Avoid Getting Your Adsense Account Terminated 14
      Monetizing Your Website With Adsense Is Profitable! 16
      2 Surefire Ways To Maximize Your Adsense Earnings 18
      The Basics On How TO Start Making Money With Adsense 20
      Using Other Peoples Info To Increase Your Adsense Cash 22
      Who Else Wants To Make Money With Adsense? 24
   Webtraffic 26
      Effectively Using Overture/Yahoo To Get Website Visitors 27
      Here's Why Paying For Your Traffic Is A Smart Move 29
      How To Generate Traffic Using Only Free Methods 31
      How To Monetize Your Traffic So You Get The Most Out Of It 33
      How To Use A Tell A Friend Script To Drive Traffic Today 35
      7 Surefire Ways To Increase Your Traffic Starting Yesterday 37
      Search Engine Optimization And Why You Gotta Use It 40
      Top 5 Ways To Generate Low Cost Website Traffic 42
      Using Google Adwords To Drive Laser Targeted Traffic 45
      Viral Marketing 101 - Not Using It Could Kill Your Business! 47
   Affiliate Marketing 49
      3 Things All Affiliate Marketers Need To Survive Online 50
      A Day In The Life Of An Affiliate Marketer 52
      Easy Profits Using PPC In Your Affiliate Marketing Business 55
      Here's How To Avoid The 3 Most Common Affiliate Mistakes 57
      Here's Why Using Camtasia Can Increase Your Affiliate Checks 59
      How To Become A Super Affiliate In Niche Markets 62
      So Many Affiliate Programs! Which One Do I Choose? 64
      Top 3 Ways To Boost Your Affiliate Commissions Overnight 66

Using Product Recommendations To Increase Your Bottom Line 68
Which Affiliate Networks To Look Out For When Promoting 70
Article Marketing 72
   3 Things You Must Do Before You Submit To Article Directories 73
   4 Things ALL Articles Must Have - Don't Forget! 75
   5 Easy Ways To Get Your Creative Juices Going 77
   6 Red Hot Tips To Get Your Articles Read 79
   Articles Are The Quickest Way To Your Customers Wallet 81
   How to Create an Outline For All of Your Article 84
   I Hate Writing Articles - Isn't There An Easier Way?! 86
   The easiest Way to Create Articles – Public Domain! 88
   Top Writers Around the World will write for you – outsourcing 90
   Writing the Resource Box so it Makes People click 92
Opt-In-List 94
   3 Quick And Easy Ways To Build A Profitable Opt In List 95
   4 Crucial Things You Need To Do To Build your List 97
   4 Ways To Get Your Opt In Subscribers To Trust You Quickly 99
   5 Things To Consider When Publishing A Newsletter 101
   7 Ways To Make Money Using Nothing More Than Your List 103
   Can You Really Use Articles To Build Your List? 105
   How To Build A List Of Eager Subscribers 107
   How To Get Your Subscribers Begging For More 109
   How To Grab Your Readers Attention With Your Subject 111
   The 3 Things To Avoid When Emailing Your List 113
25 Various Tips 115
   Affiliate Marketing: Why is it One of the Most Cost-Effective Ways to Advertise your Business 116
   Writing Articles as an Affordable Internet Marketing Method 118
   Best Internet Marketing Solutions Without Overspending 120
   Blogging: Free Internet Marketing Method 122
   How to Make Use of Cheap Internet Banner Advertising 124
   Email Marketing: Affordable Internet Marketing Technique 126
   The Best Internet Advertising is Free Internet Advertising 128
   Free Internet Marketing Methods that will Save your Internet Business 130

How to Acquire Free Web Site Promotion	132
Three Traffic Tactics that won't Cost You a Cent	134
All About Internet Advertising Methods	136
Low cost advanced website traffic tactics for everyone	138
Low Cost Advertising and Scams on the Internet	140
Aggressive Internet Marketing Made Possible	142
Affordable Advertising Agencies	144
Low Cost Internet Advertising Solution versus Conventional Advertising	146
Internet Marketing Strategies that Won't Hurt Your Savings Much	148
Tool Talk: All about internet marketing tools	150
Determining Quality and Low Cost Pay per Click Internet Advertising Services	152
Effective SEO Comes Cheap	154
Two Basic Parts of a Low Cost Web Site Promotion	156
Effective SEO Comes Cheap	158
"Pay-Per Click" Ad Campaign: Earn More by Spending Less"	160
Free Website Promotion...Why Not?	161
"Maximum Exposure on Low Cost Internet Ad"	163
(Make the most of a low cost Internet advertising method)	163

Google Adsense

3 Reasons Why Adsense Is Essential For Content Sites

To know why Adsense is essential for your content sites is to know first how this works.

The concept is really simple, if you think about it. The publisher or the webmaster inserts a java script into a certain website. Each time the page is accessed, the java script will pull advertisements from the Adsense program. The ads that are targeted should therefore be related to the content that is contained on the web page serving the ad. If a visitor clicks on an advertisement, the webmaster serving the ad earns a portion of the money that the advertiser is paying the search engine for the click.

The search engine is the one handling all the tracking and payments, providing an easy way for webmasters to display content-sensitive and targeted ads without having the hassle to solicit advertisers, collect funds, monitor the clicks and statistics which could be a time-consuming task in itself. It seems that there is never a shortage of advertisers in the program from which the search engine pulls the Adsense ads. Also webmasters are less concerned by the lack of information search engines are providing and are more focused in making cash from these search engines.

The first reason why Adsense is essential for content sites is because it already has come a long way in understanding the needs of publishers and webmasters. Together with its continuous progression is the appearance of more advanced system that allows full ad customization. Webmasters are given the chance to choose from many different types of text ad formats to better complement their website and fit their webpage layout.

The different formatting enables the site owners the possibility of more click through from visitors who may or may not be aware of what they are clicking on. It can also appeal to the people visiting thus make them take that next step of looking up what it is all about. This way the people behind the Adsense will get their content read and making profit in the process.

The second reason is the ability of the Adsense publishers to track not only how their sites are progressing but also the earnings based on the webmaster-defined channels. The recent improvements in the search engines gives webmasters the capability to monitor how their ads are performing using customizable reports that has the capacity to detail page impressions, clicks and click-through rates. Webmasters and publishers can now track specific ad formats, colors and pages within a website. Trends are also easily spotted.

With the real-time reporting at hand, the effectiveness of the changes made will be assessed quickly. There would be time to sort out the contents that people are making the most clicks on. The ever-changing demands would be met while generating cash for the webmasters and publishers. The more flexible tools are also allowing webmasters to group web pages by URL, domain, ad type or category, which will provide them some accurate insight on which pages, ads and domains are performing best.

The last and final reason is that the advertisers have realized the benefits associated having their ads served on targeted websites. Thus increasing the possibility that a prospective web surfer will have an interest in their product and services. All because of the content and its constant maintenance. As opposed to those who are no using Adsense in their sites, they are given the option of having other people do their content for them, giving them the benefit of having successful and money-generating web sites.

Adsense is all about targeted content, the more targeted your content is, the more target the search engines' ads will be. There are some web masters and publishers who are focused more on their site contents and how best to maintain them rather than the cash that the ads will generate for them. This is the part where the effectiveness is working its best.

There was a time when people were not yet aware of the money to be achieved from advertisements. The cash generated only came into existence when the webmasters and publishers realized how they can make Adsense be that generator. In those days, the content were the most important factors that is taken quite seriously. It still is. With the allure of money, of course.

5 Ways To Improve Your Adsense Earnings

If webmasters want to monetize their websites, the great way to do it is through Adsense. There are lots of webmasters struggling hard to earn some good money a day through their sites. But then some of the "geniuses" of them are enjoying hundreds of dollars a day from Adsense ads on their websites. What makes these webmasters different from the other kind is that they are different and they think out of the box.

The ones who have been there and done it have quite some useful tips to help those who would want to venture into this field. Some of these tips have boosted quite a lot of earnings in the past and is continuously doing so.

Here are some 5 proven ways on how best to improve your Adsense earnings.

1. Concentrating on one format of Adsense ad. The one format that worked well for the majority is the Large Rectangle (336X280). This same format have the tendency to result in higher CTR, or the click-through rates. Why choose this format out of the many you can use? Basically because the ads will look like normal web links, and people, being used to clicking on them, click these types of links. They may or may not know they are clicking on your Adsense but as long as there are clicks, then it will all be for your advantage.

2. Create a custom palette for your ads. Choose a color that will go well with the background of your site. If your site has a white background, try to use white as the color of your ad border and background. The idea to patterning the colors is to make the Adsense look like it is part of the web pages. Again, This will result to more clicks from people visiting your site.

3. Remove the Adsense from the bottom pages of your site and put them at the top. Do not try to hide your Adsense. Put them in the place where people can see them quickly. You will be amazed how the difference between Adsense locations can make when you see your earnings.

4. Maintain links to relevant websites. If you think some sites are better off than the others, put your ads there and try to maintaining and managing them. If there is already lots of Adsense put into that certain site, put yours on top of all of them. That way visitor will see your ads first upon browsing into that site.

5. Try to automate the insertion of your Adsense code into the webpages using SSI (or server side included). Ask your web administrator if your server supports SSI or not. How do you do it? Just save your Adsense code in a text file, save it as "adsense text", and upload it to the root directory of the web server. Then using SSI, call the code on other pages. This tip is a time saver especially for those who are using automatic page generators to generate pages on their website.

These are some of the tips that have worked well for some who want to generate hundreds and even thousands on their websites. It is important to know though that ads are displayed because it fits the interest of the people viewing them. So focusing on a specific topic should be your primary purpose because the displays will be especially targeted on a topic that persons will be viewing already.

Note also that there are many other Adsense sharing the same topic as you. It is best to think of making a good ad that will be somewhat different and unique than the ones already done. Every clickthrough that visitors make is a point for you so make every click count by making your Adsense something that people will definitely click on.

Tips given by those who have boosted their earnings are just guidelines they want to share with others. If they have somehow worked wonders to some, maybe it can work wonders for you too. Try them out into your ads and see the result it will bring.

If others have done it, there is nothing wrong trying it out for yourself.

Don't Get Caught With Google Adsense Click Fraud

Many web site owners are getting their Google Adsense account terminated when they have done nothing wrong to deserve the punishment. Considering the money that they are getting from Adsense, they would certainly want to get back into it.

Considering the money to be made with Adsense, it is no wonder that they would want to get back into it.

It is that same consideration why the Google Adsense click fraud is thought of and why many people are getting into it.

Click fraud is the act of clicking on ads for the purpose of costing the advertiser money. It is simply the same as paying out cash for false leads. Many people website owners are aware of this fraud and are sharing the same sentiment that this is the one big problem that Adsense is facing.

How do you prevent being involved in this fraud?

Majority of web hosts are offering access logs. Once this is offered to you, it is necessary that you hand it over to Google as well. This allows them to look for any suspicious activity on your site. Problems like this are very serious and giving it to them is saying that you would want to help them in any way you can in solving the problem.

It can also help if you have a click monitoring software. If you do not have one yet, you should try and get one. There is absolutely no major factor preventing you from having one because most of this software is free.

As usual, all the information you have received should be turned over to Google. This is showing Google that you too are fighting against click frauds and is in no way a part of it.

Study your server logs and watch for any activity that seems suspicious. Report anything that you may find odd, may it big or small thing.

You may want to consider disabling ads for your own IP address and local geographic area. This will certainly prevent accidents and will not make Google mistake another user as you. You can do through a htaccess file. This will avoid Google mistaking as clicking on your own ads and be kicked out because of it.

Keep your Adsense off on pop ups and pop unders. Your ads should not be displayed on content sites that promote illegal activity or tampering of the legal rights of other people or business. Included in this are the content that is considered adult and gambling ones. If you think that you may be breaking this rule, immediately remove your content or Adsense from the web page.

Be truthful and confess up to Google about times when you might have clicked on your own as, whether accidentally or intentionally. Or the times when you have done something that is against the Terms of Service that they are implementing. Be honest about anything that you may have done that is wrong. Confessing is way better than Google learning about it eventually. It would mean eventual termination and no getting back what you have worked so hard for.

Do not tell your family or friends about Adsense on your website. Chances are they may start clicking on them to help you make money without you knowing it. They may be doing more harm to you than help by trying it in the first place.

If ever someone you know chanced upon your Adsense, make sure they understand that they cannot click on your ads under any circumstances. It would be wise to brief them on important things about Adsense and what not to do with them.

Most pay per click networks have different measures in hand to protect website owners against click frauds. Other search engines can track more than 50 data points, IP address, browser's information, user's session info and pattern recognition. They also have "systems" available that detects fraud. Not to mention the specialized teams monitoring how things are going and helping advertisers stop click frauds.

Google offers suggestion on how to avoid click fraud. Using "negative keywords" can be used to keep your Adsense showing on products and services that are in no way related to yours. Adding tracking URLs to your links so you can track the traffic coming from Google.

Do not be caught in the Google click fraud. Be aware and be wary.

Google Adsense - The Easiest Money To Make Online?

For the last couple of months, Google Adsense has dominated forums, discussions and newsletters all over the Internet. Already, there are tales of fabulous riches to be made and millions made by those who are just working from home. It seems that Google Adsense have already dominated the internet marketing business and is now considered the easiest way to making money online.

The key to success with Adsense is the placing of ads on pages that are receiving high traffic for high demand keywords. The higher the cost-per-click to the advertiser, the more you will receive per click from your site. Obviously, it does not pay to target low cost-per-click keywords and place them on pages that do not receive hits.

With all the people getting online and clicking away everyday, it is no wonder why Google Adsense has become an instant hit.

For some who are just new to this market, it would be a blow to their pride knowing that their homepage is buried somewhere in the little ads promoting other people's services. But then, when they get the idea that they are actually earning more money that way, all doubts and skepticism is laid to rest.

There are two major, and clever, factors that some successful webmaster and publishers are learning to blend together in order to make money easier using Adsense.

1. Targeting high traffic pages on your website. If you check on your logs, you will discover that many of your visitors are taking advantage of the free affiliate marketing resources and ebooks that you are offering on your site. In simple words, your ads are working effectively and are generating more clicks. It also means more money for you.

2. Placing Adsense links on pages that are producing little, or better yet, no profit. By placing Adsense on a free resources page, you will reduce the amount of potential customers being lost to other sites. Tricky, but effective nonetheless.

When learned to work effectively, these two factors are actually a good source of producing a minimal amount of revenue from a high traffic page. Many people are using this strategy to pick up some extra and cash with Adsense. This is also especially rewarding to informational sites that focus their efforts on delivering powerful affiliate link free content to their visitors. Now they can gain a monetary return on their services.

With the many techniques that people are now learning on how to make the easiest money by their Adsense, it is not surprising that Google is trying everything to update and polish their Adsense in order to maintain their good image.

The possibility of adding is 2nd tier in Adsense is not impossible. With all the people spending more time in their Adsense now and still more getting into this line of marketing, there is no doubt about the many new improvements yet to be made. Imagine the smiles on the faces of the webmasters and publishers all around the world if ever they sign up for sub-affiliates and double or even triple the amount that they are already earning.

The one particularly handy money-making feature that is available with Adsense now is the ability to filter out up to 200 urls. These gives webmasters the option to block out low value offers from their pages as well as competitors to their websites. Talk about taking only those that are advantageous and discarding the ones that seem "useless".

With Google Adsense, the possibilities are limitless. Yet there is also the possibility of someone taking advantage of the easy money process that this internet marketing is doing. If you think more about it, these negative factors may force Google to break down and thrash Adsense in the process. If that happens, people would have to go back to the old ways of internet marketing that does not make money online as easy as Adsense.

For now, however, Google Adsense is here to stay. As long as there are people wanting to earn some easy cash online just using their talents, the future ahead is looking good. Besides with all the strict guidelines that Google is enforcing over Adsense, it will take awhile for the Adsense privileges to be spammed and even terminated.

How To Avoid Getting Your Adsense Account Terminated

Google, being the undisputable leader in search engines from then until now, is placing a high importance on the quality and relevancy of its search engines. Most especially now that the company is public property. In order to keep the shareholders and users of its engines happy, the quality of the returned results are given extreme importance.

For this same reason, doing the wrong things in the Adsense and other forms of advertisements, whether intentionally or unintentionally, will result in a severe penalty, may get you banned and even have your account terminated. Nothing like a good action taken to keep wrongdoers from doing the same things over again.

So for those who are thinking of getting a career in Adsense, do not just think of the strategies you will be using to generate more earnings. Consider some things first before you actually get involved.

Hidden texts. Filling your advertisement page with texts to small to read, has the same color as the background and using css for the sole purpose of loading them with rich keywords content and copy will earn you a penalty award that is given to those who are hiding links.

Page cloaking. There is a common practice of using browser or bot sniffers to serve the bots of a different page other than the page your visitors will see. Loading a page with a bot that a human user will never see is a definite no-no. This is tricking them to click on something that you want but they may not want to go to.

Multiple submissions. Submitting multiple copies of your domain and pages is another thing to stay away from. For example, trying to submit a URL of an Adsense as two separate URL's is the same as inviting trouble and even termination. Likewise, this is a reason to avoid auto submitters for those who are receiving submissions. Better check first if your domain is submitted already an a certain search engine before you try to submit to it again. If you see it there, then move on. No point contemplating whether to try and submit there again.

Link farms. Be wary of who and what are you linking your Adsense to. The search engines know that you cannot control your links in. But you can certainly control what you link to. Link farming has always been a rotten apple in the eyes of search engines, especially Google. That is reason enough to try and avoid them. Having a link higher than 100 on a single page will classify you as a link farm so try and not to make them higher than that.

Page rank for sale. If you have been online for quite some time, you will notice that there are some sites selling their PR links or trading them with other sites. If you are doing this, expect a ban anytime in the future. It is okay to sell ads or gain the link. But doing it on direct advertisement of your page rank is a way to get on search engines bad side.

Doorways. This is similar to cloaking pages. The common practice of a page loaded with choice keyword ads aimed at redirecting visitors to another "user-friendly" page is a big issue among search engines. There are many seo firms offering this kind of services. Now that you know what they actually are, try to avoid them at all costs.

Multiple domains having the same content. In case you are not aware of it, search engines look at domains IP's, registry dates and many others. Having multiple domains having the same exact content is not something you can hide from them. The same goes with content multiplied many times on separate pages, sub domains and forwarding multiple domains to the same content.

Many of the above techniques apply to most search engines and is not entirely for Google only. By having a mind set that you are building your Adsense together with your pages for the human users and not for bots, you can be assured of the great things for your ads and sites.

Not to mention avoiding the wrath of the search engines and getting your Adsense and site account terminated altogether.

Monetizing Your Website With Adsense Is Profitable!

How do you maximize your site?

By earning some few dollars per click from displaying Adsense ads on it. Many are now realizing that good money is made from this source of revenue. Try the simple mathematical computation of multiplying those clicks for every page on your website and you get a summation of earnings equivalent to a monthly residual income with that little effort you have made.

Google Adsense is a fast and easy way for website publishers of all sizes to display relevant and text-based Google ads on their website's content pages and earn money in the process. The ads displayed are related to what your users are looking for on your site. This is the main reason why you both can monetize and enhance your content pages using Adsense.

How much you will be earning will depend on how much the advertisers are willing to pay. It will depend also on the keywords required. If the keywords the advertiser have chosen are in high demand, you could receive more dollars per click. On the other hand, low demand keywords will earn you just a few cents per click.

How can you start making profits out of your website using Adsense?

1. Sign up for an Adsense account. It will only take a few minutes of your time.

2. When the site is accepted, you will be receiving a clip code to include in your web pages. You can insert this code on as many pages or web sites that you want. The AdWords will start appearing immediately after.

3. You will be earning a few cents or some dollars per click when someone starts clicking on the AdWords displayed on any of your web pages. Trying to earn false revenues by repetitively clicking on your own ads is a no-no. This will result in a penalty or the possibility of your site being eliminated. The money you have already earned may be lost because of this.

4. View your statistics. Adsense earnings can be checked anytime by logging into your web site account.

Once you got your account working, you may still want to pattern them to the many sites that are earning more money than you are. It is important to note that there are factors affecting how your website will perform and the amount of money it will give you.

It is a common practice that when a site earning money, the tendency is for the owner to want to make more out of what they are getting already. It usually takes some time combined with trial and error to attain what you want for your Adsense contents.

Time and some important factors that you can practice and use.

How do you increase your Adsense earnings?

1. Choose one topic per page. It is best to write a content for your page with just a few targeted phrases. The search engine will then serve ads that are more relevant which will then result in higher clickthoughs.

2. Using white space around your ad. This can make your ad stand out from the rest of your page so visitors can spot them easily. There are also other choices of colors you can use, provided by search engines, which can harmonize the color of your ad with the web page color.

3. Test your ad placement. It is recommended to use the vertical format that runs down the side of the web page to get more positive results. You can also try both horizontal and vertical formats for a certain period of time to see which one will give you better results.

4. More content-based pages. Widen the theme of your website by creating pages that focus more on your keyword phrases. This will optimize the pages for the search engines. It can not only attract traffic but also make them more relevant for the AdWords to be displayed.

5. Site Build It. This is the perfect tool to be used for creating lots of Adsense revenues. Site Build It has all the tools necessary to quickly achieve a keyword-rich site that can rank high in the search engines. This will also produce a flow of traffic to your site of highly targeted visitors.

2 Surefire Ways To Maximize Your Adsense Earnings

Most webmasters know that Adsense generates a sizeable source of additional advertising income. That is why most of them use it to go after high paying keywords. They have with them the lists that tells what the keywords are and have already used various methods of identifying them. And yet, after putting up these supposed-to-be high paying keywords into their pages, the money they expected to come rolling in is not really coming in.

What is it that they are doing wrong?

Having the pages is with the proper keywords is one thing. But driving visitors to those pages is another matter and often the factor that is lacking.

The thing is, to get visitors to your high paying keyword pages, you need to optimize your site navigation.

Stop for a moment and think about how visitors are using your website. After a visitor has landed on a certain page, they have the tendency to click on another page that sounds interesting. They get there because of the other links that appears on a page that they initially landed on. This is site navigation. It is all about enabling visitors to move about your site. And one way of maximizing your Adsense earnings.

A typical website have menu links on each page. The wording on these links is what grabs a visitor's attention and gets them to click on one of the links that will take them to another page of that website. Links that have "free' or "download" are oftentimes good attention-grabbers.

This navigation logic can also be applied to driving traffic to your high paying pages. There are some websites that are getting a lot of traffic from search engines, but have low earnings. The trick is to try and use come cleverly labeled links to get the visitors off that pages and navigate them to the higher earning ones. This is one great way of turning real cheap clicks to real dollars.

Before you begin testing if this same style will work for you and you website, you need to have two things. Something to track and compare and some high earning pages you want to funnel your site traffic to. An option is to select a few of your frequently visited pages. This is ensuring fast result to come by.

Now, the next thing to do is think of ways to get visitors viewing a particular page to try and click on the link that will take them to your high earning pages. Come up with a catchy description for that link. Come up with a catchy and unique description for the link. Think of something that people do not get to see everyday. That will trigger their curiosity enough to try and see what that was all about.

You can also use graphics to grab your readers' attention. There is no limitation to what you can do to make your link noticeable. If you are after the success of your site, you will do everything it takes just to achieve that goal. Just be creative. As far as many Adsense advertisers are concerned, there are no written and unwritten laws to follow regarding what they write. Just as long as you do not overstep the guidelines of the search engines, then go for it.

Also remember that it is all about location, location and location. Once the perfect attention grabbing description has been achieved, you have to identify the perfect spot on your page to position that descriptive link to your high paying page.

There is nothing wrong with visiting other websites to see how they are going about maximizing their site navigation. "Hot pages" or "Most read" lists are very common and overly used already. Get to know the ones that many websites are using and do not try to imitate them.

Another way of doing it is to try and use different texts on different pages. That way you will see the ones that work and what does not. Try to mix things around also. Put links on top and sometimes on the bottom too. This is how you go about testing which ones get more clicks and which ones are being ignored.

Let the testing begin. Testing and tracking until you find the site navigation style that works best for you site.

The Basics On How TO Start Making Money With Adsense

Adsense is considered as one of the most powerful tool in a website publisher's arsenal. It enables a person to monetize their sites easily. If used properly, it can generate a very large and healthy income for them. However if you are not using them rightly and just maximizing the income you squeeze from it, you are actually leaving a lot of money on the table. Something all people hate doing.

How you can start earning money with Adsense can be done easily and quickly. You will be amazed at the results you will be getting in such a short period of time.

Start by writing some quality content articles which are also keyword incorporated. There are a lot of people given the gift of being good with words. Writing comes easy for them. Why not make it work in such a way that you will be earning some extra cash in the process.

There are actually three steps to put into mind before you begin writing your ads and having an effective Adsense.

Keyword search. Find some popular subjects, keywords or phrase. Select the ones which you think has more people clicking through. This is actually a keyword selector and suggestion tool that some sites are offering to those who are just their Adsense business.

Writing articles. Start writing original content with keywords from the topics that you have achieved in your search. Take note that search engines are taking pride in the quality of their articles and what you will be writing should keep up with their demands.

Quality content site. Build a quality content site incorporated with Adsense ads that is targeting the subject and keywords of your articles and websites. This is where all that you've done initially will go to and this is also where they will prove their worth to you.

The proper positioning of your ads should be done with care. Try to position your ads where surfers are most likely to click on them. According to research, the one place that surfers look first when they visit a certain site is the top left. The reason behind this is not known. Maybe it is because some of the most useful search engine results are at the top of all other rankings. So visitors tend to look in that same place when browsing through other sites.

Some of those who are just starting at this business may think they are doing pretty well already and thinking that their clickthrough rates and CPM figures are quite healthy. However, there are more techniques and styles to generate more clicks to double your earnings. By knowing these techniques and working them to your advantage, you will realize that you will be getting three times more than other people who have been previously doing what they are doing.

Finally, Adsense has some excellent tracking statistics that allows webmasters and publishers to track their results across a number of site on a site by site, page by page, or any other basis you wanted. You should be aware oft his capability and make the most of it because it is one powerful tool that will help you find out which ads are performing best. This way, you can fine tune your Adsense ads and focus more on the ones being visited the most rather than those who are being ignored.

Another thing you should know. Banners and skyscrapers are dead. Ask the experts. So better forget about banners and skyscrapers. Surfers universally ignore these kinds of ad formats. The reason behind this is that they are recognized as an advert and advert are rarely of any interest that's why people ignore them.

To really start making money with Adsense, you should have a definite focus on what you wanted to achieve and how you will go about achieving them. As with any other kind of business ventures, time is needed coupled with patience.

Do not just ignore your site and your Adsense once you have finished accomplishing them. Spare some time, even an hour, making adjustments to the Adsense ads on your sites to quickly trigger your Adsense income.

Give it a try and you would not regret having gotten into Adsense in the first place.

Using Other Peoples Info To Increase Your Adsense Cash

Adsense is really making a huge impact on the affiliate marketing industry nowadays. Because of this, weak affiliate merchants have the tendency to die faster than ever and ad networks will be going to lose their customers quickly.

If you are in a losing rather than winning in the affiliate program you are currently into, maybe it is about time to consider going into the Adsense marketing and start earning some real cash.

Google is readily providing well written and highly relevant ads that are closely chosen to match the content on your pages. You do not have to look for them yourselves as the search engine will be the doing the searching for you from other people's source.

You do not have to spend time in choosing different kind of ads for different pages. And no codes to mess around for different affiliate programs.

You will be able to concentrate on providing good and quality content, as the search engines will be the ones finding the best ads in which to put your pages on.

You are still allowed to add Adsense ads even if you already have affiliate links on your site. It is prohibited, however, to imitate the look and feel of the Google ads for your affiliate links.

You can filter up to 200 URLs. That gives you a chance to block ads for the sites that do not meet your guidelines. You can also block competitors. Though it is unavoidable that Adsense may be competing for some space on web sites that all other revenues are sharing.

Owners of small sites are allowed to plug a bit of a code into their sites and instantly have relevant text ads that appeal to your visitors appear instantly into your pages. If you own many sites, you only need to apply once. It makes up for having to apply to many affiliate programs.

The only way to know how much you are already earning is to try and see. If you want out, all you have to do is remove the code from your site.

The payment rates can vary extremely. The payment you will be receiving per click depends on how much advertisers are paying per click to advertise with the use of the AdWords. Advertisers can pay as little as 5 cents and as high as $10-12, sometimes even more than that too. You are earning a share of that money generated.

If your results remain stagnant, it can help if you try and build simple and uncluttered pages so that the ads can catch the visitor's eyes more. It sometimes pay to differ from the usual things that people are doing already. It is also a refreshing sight for your visitor once they see something different for a change.

Publishers also have the option of choosing to have their ads displayed only on a certain site or sites. It is also allowed to have them displayed on a large network of sites. The choice would be depending on what you think will work best for your advantage.

To get an idea if some Adsense ads you see on the search engines has your pages, try to find web pages that have similar material to the content you are planning to create and look up their Adsense ads.

It is important to note that you cannot choose certain topics only. If you do this, search engines will not place Adsense ads on your site and you will be missing out a great opportunity in making hundreds and even thousands of dollars cash.

It is still wise to look at other people's information and format your Adsense there. Just think about it as doing yourself a favor by not having to work too hard to know what content to have.

Topic to be avoided includes gambling, firearms, ammunition, tobacco or drugs. If you are being offered more cash in exchange of doing Adsense with these kinds, it is just like signing your own termination paper.

With all the information that people need in your hands already, all you have to do is turn them as your profits. It all boils down to a gain and gain situation both for the content site owners and the webmasters or publishers.

Make other people's matter your own and starting earning some extra cash.

Who Else Wants To Make Money With Adsense?

Fact number 1: Kids in high school are making thousands of dollars every month with Adsense.

Fact number 2: Housewives, retirees, mom and dads, who are just staying at home and have never made a dime on the internet have created full-time incomes by simply placing Adsense ads on their web site or blog.

These are just some of the "super Adsense earners". You may have already heard about their story for they are among the few who are on their way to making millions worth of cash just by promoting Adsense sites.

Anyone, any age and gender can become money generating Adsense publishers as long as they what it takes. How does one go about this Internet advertising?

Writing articles for Adsense is the way to do it. Using the right keywords in your articles and having Google ads on a certain site has become the most profitable way of marketing that anybody can get into. No experience and level of education needed. If you are not using this strategy, or may not be aware of it in the first place, chances are you may be losing thousands of dollars worth of extra income and still do not know it yet.

This is one of the many reasons why writing original quality content articles is now the latest in marketing buzz. Content and links. When combined together becomes a really powerful tool to a successful web site and richer individuals. Many internet marketing professionals are already aware of the value of an original quality content and how using keywords can drive targeted traffic into their sites from the search engines.

So why don't all these web site owners write and submit their own articles if that is what is important?

The simple and understandable answer is that it takes time to write articles, submit them and get targeted traffic to their websites. That is why they get the services of those who can spares sometime to write the articles that would cater to their site purpose but still turn out as a good quality and unique piece of work.

To get into the Adsense marketing business and start earning some good cash, ask yourself. Did you enjoy writing when you were in school? If you answer yes to this question, you already have an initial advantage over most internet marketing business owners that wants to make money online and doing it at home.

With the boom in the Adsense market comes the need for sites to want fresh, quality and original keyword rich content. This way, web site owners can have a steady supply of articles with the proper keywords that they relate to their site contents. The result of this is seen in the sites page rank when indexed by the search engines. Which, in turn, gets moreAdsense ads to show above, below or next to the article on their website with targeted traffic.

What do people have to do?

Write quality and original content, keyword or phrase rich articles with links to your website in the resource box. Then build a website or web page with targeted keyword or phrase rich original content for the targeted traffic that originates from the articles you wrote. Finally, you will have a Google Adsense ads that are targeted to your keyword or phrase rich original content site where visitors will get to visit when they come looking for information.

A win-win situation if you think more about it. A favor for persons looking for quality content and information. For the persons writing the original content articles. And the person with the quality original content rich website. Of course, the search engines and its advertisers are getting targeted traffic and sales but so what? As long as you are getting something in your favor, it does not really matter what the others are getting for themselves.

So who else wants to start earning money with Adsense. You. Everyone. Anybody. Internet marketing has many opportunities wide open for this people. Writing articles and using Adsense for your kind of internet marketing strategy is one sure way of getting a piece of that action and cash.

Better not be left behind the many making millions already.

Webtraffic

Effectively Using Overture/Yahoo To Get Website Visitors

Overture or now known as Yahoo because of Yahoo's takeover, was the original inventor of the use of the P4P or Pay for Performance. Overture saw that the internet was fast becoming the easiest and most convenient way to shop, and advertising was going to hit at an all time high because of the many businesses in the arena.

To get a person to go to a site than others, it needs to be very visible. Providing ads that could direct potential consumers and costumers to their site would allow them to have an increase in traffic as well as sales. Yahoo provides a service that can put a site or company's ad in their sites that can be shown when certain keywords are inputted.

Yahoo offers a chance for any company to increase their traffic by using their services. With more people being aware of your site, there would be more traffic and visitors to your site given the chance to view your pages as well as your products. With even a small percentage of successful sales, with a high traffic volume this could still be a substantial figure for your company.

Getting a consistent substantial flow of website visitors is every company's goal. Many methods are devised and utilized to ensure that there would be more people to boost the sales and to be aware of the existence of such a product or service. Website visitors are potentially the life blood of your internet based business.

Yahoo/Overture utilizes the same principle as Google's Adwords. In fact, they are very similar to each other that they use keyword and keyword phrase searches and to determine which ads to show per search. When a person types in a keyword or keyword phrase to search for anything, the search engines gives out the results in a page. Then at the right side of the page, you will see selected ads that have paid for their ads to be viewed with certain keywords and keyword phrases searched.

For example, Lets say you run a car parts retail/wholesale site. You choose keywords that can prompt or trigger your ads to be shown in the page when a keyword is searched. When a search engine user types in Honda Accord, your ad may come up if you have designated that as one of your keywords. You don't need to fully optimize your site with Search Engine Optimization methods and techniques.

While some labor so hard to make their site one of the high ranking sites per keyword search, you get the chance to be on the top of the list or at least in the first page of a search result increasing your chance to be clicked on. With that, you drive traffic and website visitors to your site a lot faster.

You will have to pony up some cash when using this service though. There are different ways Yahoo/Overture will charge you. It may be in the number of Keywords or Keyword phrases your ad uses or in the many times your ad is clicked on. Others offer many other services like having your ad show up not only in the search engine pages but also with some third party sites.

Third party sites support ads that have the same theme or niche as them. With more areas your ad is shown, you increase the chances of people knowing about your site or product. With more website visitors you increase the sales of your site which makes your investment with your ads a wise one.

With so many competitions in the internet based businesses, it is necessary to take a huge leap forward from the pack by advertising. Yahoo/Overture will be a great place to start. Many have utilized their services and have reaped the rewards of this decision. It's a marketing strategy that will increase your website visitors as well as increase your sales resulting to profit.

It takes money to make money, while there are some methods that are basically low cost or free, using a marketing service such as what Yahoo/Overture offers will provide results faster and on a larger scale. Many businesses have learned this the hard way, don't be counted with them.

Here's Why Paying For Your Traffic Is A Smart Move

There are so many success stories you will hear about businesses making it good in the internet. The troubling thing is, there are maybe a tenfold or even a hundredfold of stories contradictory to theirs. Many have unsuccessfully launched a business enterprise that is internet based but only a handful shall succeed.

Is this through luck? That is even more remote. It takes good business sense and a lot of help and team effort. Most importantly, it is the eagerness to succeed and the determination to learn and the willingness to invest in a lot of hard work and some money.

The Very Basic

Like Neo, traffic is "The One". Without traffic, all your effort would just go to waste. Every business needs customers, without them you wouldn't have anyone to sell your products to. In the internet world traffic is the walk in customer. The more traffic you have the more people would be able to sell your products to.

But like any business that's in every corner building or in the mall, not everyone that goes in will buy, but the greater of number that do come in to browse your merchandise, the greater number of people that will buy your products. It is a simple and known fact.

But, how do you get traffic, traffic large enough that could make a small percentage of eventual buyers enough to make a good profit. Many big companies generate traffic of tens of thousands a day and a measly ten to fifteen percent actually buys, but that small percentage is enough to provide them with good business.

Many of these success stories get their traffic from paying others. Yes that's right; you have to spend money to make money. Advertising is the key. The more people that knows that your site exists; the more people would of course go to your site, that's common sense.

While there are many ways that can get you advertising for free, this do not generate the same high volume as those methods that are getting paid. These paid advertisements include advertising schemes by Google and Yahoo.

The Value of Searches

The search and will be the easiest and fastest medium in finding what a person needs in the internet. Search engines have been very popular because they provide a vital service to many people. They are free and easy to use. With this popularity, they get many visitors and clicks that they are the most common sites that people go to. It is easy to understand why so many companies would pay to advertise with these search engines.

Search engines provide information to the millions of users that they have each day. They provide links to many sites that a user may be looking for. If your sites link pop up in the high ranks of the search results page, you get a great chance that they will go to your site. While search engine optimization is a cheaper and low cost way to get your site a high rank, paying for advertisements will ensure that you will be on the top ranks.

When you pay for your advertisements, it is like paying for your traffic. This may sound like not such a good idea, but the payoffs would tell a different story. When you pay for your traffic, you are guaranteed of a consistent traffic flow to your site. You will never go with an empty sales day.

Paying for your Traffic

Usually, you will be charged with the number of hits a link gets when your ads is clicked, this is called pay per click. For some search engines, you will be charged with the number of times your ad shows up when a certain keyword or keyword phrase is searched. It is imperative that you have good keyword content in your ad. There are many tools that aid you in using the right keyword for the right moment.

All the money you spend in paying for your traffic will not be for naught. You will get an impressive boost in traffic which will also result to a great boost in your sales figures. Paying for your traffic would be a really good idea and you will get all the benefits it has to offer.

How To Generate Traffic Using Only Free Methods

Putting up a company would of course require a lot of things, to get straight to the point, you need a capital. To make money requires money as well. But of course, with the versatility the internet offers, there are many ways you could find that could help optimize the potential of your site or business in generating traffic.

While there are ways to jumpstart your traffic flows, many sites don't have the resources that others have to generate more traffic for your site. Well, you don't have to spend a cent; all you need is the proper mindset and a lot of eagerness. You also must have the drive and perseverance to do hard work and research to generate more traffic for your site.

How sweet it is to have more traffic for your site without spending a single cent. Now it's a sure thing that many sites have articles that offer tips and guidelines in how to generate traffic using only free methods. Because it is possible, you don't need to speed a single cent, it may take time, to say honestly, I'm not going to beat around the bush with you. You get better chances by paying for your advertisements, but at least you get a fighting chance with some of these free methods I'm about to tell you.

Take advantage of online forums and online communities. The great thing about forums and online communities is that you can target a certain group that fits the certain demographic that you are looking for. You can discuss about lots of things about the niche that you represent or offer. Another great advantage is that you know what you are getting into and you will be prepared.

With online communities and forums you can build a reputation for your company. Show them what you are made of and wow them with your range of expertise about the subject, with that you can build a reputation and build trust with the people in your expertise and knowledge.

You can also make use of newsletters. Provide people with a catalog of your products and interesting and entertaining articles. If you make it really interesting and entertaining, more people will sign up for your newsletter and recommend it to other people. The more people who signs up for your newsletter, the more people there will be that will go to your site increasing your traffic.

Another great idea is trading links with other sites. You don't have to spend a cent. All you have to do is reach an agreement with another webmaster. With exchanging links, the efforts both sites do will benefit both sites. Every traffic that goes to the site could potentially click on the link of your site and visit your site as well. This works well especially when both sites feature the same niche.

Write articles that could pique the attention of people that have interest in your product. Try writing articles that will provide tips and guides to other aficionados. Writing articles that provide good service and knowledge to other people would provide the necessary mileage your traffic flow needs.

Many sites offer free submission and posting of your articles. When people find interest in your articles they have a good chance of following the track by finding out where the article originated. Include a link or a brief description of your company with the article and there's a great probability that they will go to your site.

Write good content for your site. Many search engines track down the keywords and keyword phrases your site uses and how they are used. It is not a requirement that a content should be done by a professional content writer. You could do your on but you have to make content for your site that is entertaining as well as informational. It should provide certain requirements as well as great quality.

Generally, internet users use search engines to find what they are looking for. Search engines in return use keyword searching in aiding their search results. With the right keywords, you could get high rankings in search engine results without the costs.

All of these methods and more will drive more traffic to your site for free. All it takes is a bit of effort and extended man hours. Learn all you can about the methods depicted here and you will soon have a site with a great traffic flow without the usual costs that come with it.

How To Monetize Your Traffic So You Get The Most Out Of It

Establishing your own E-commerce site is not like what it used to be. There are thousands of competition that is all too willing to get a bigger share of the pie. Every scheme and method you can find to augment your sales would be very beneficial.

We have got to admit to ourselves. Most of us are into it for the money. We are not going to waste our time and effort just for the fun of it. Many sites would not wait until hell freezes over just to see their profits. While there are some who takes things lightly there are always those who would rather see profit any given day.

It is common knowledge that without traffic we have no business. Like any business, without any customers you don't get sales. Traffic represents all the people that gets a chance to see what you have to offer. The more people who see your products the more people there would be to buy them.

Nobody puts up an E-commerce site that doesn't expect profit. We have a startup capital that needs to be regained. With a consistent traffic, we at least have a fighting chance to achieve that probability. Monetizing your traffic would optimize your chances of making the best out of it.

Making Money out of your Traffic

The best and most proven method of making a profit out of your traffic is using advertising. The internet generates hundreds of thousands upon hundred of thousands of traffic everyday. Most of them are searching for something. While some are just looking for information there is also a good percentage that is looking for something that they need.

The internet has proven to be a very reliable source in finding what was deemed to be a very unsearchable product. The internet has made the world a smaller place; you can advertise a product from the depths of Istanbul and still find a buyer from the center of Philadelphia.

Generating traffic is not an easy task. You have to contend with a great number of sites to generate a good number of traffic flow. But if done successfully this could open up a Pandora's Box of possibilities. One of the benefits is monetizing your traffic flow.

So, to get to the core of it the more traffic you generate the more likely you are considered as a desirable, desirable, in a sense that a good traffic flowing site is easily convertible to profit. Basically traffic equals profit. Advertising is the name of the game; with the good advertising scheme you can use your traffic flow to your advantage.

When you have good traffic you have a good number of potential customers, customers that are willing to pour money into your coffers. Other than that these are also traffic that can be redirected to sponsored links that are willing to pay you for a sizeable portion of the traffic that you have generated.

This scheme is called "pay-per-click". With every click a visitor of your site makes on an advertised link you will be paid. The more traffic you generate and the more clicks that happens would spell to more profits.

Affiliate Programs

Another method of monetizing your traffic are affiliate programs. You can link up with other tried and tested sites and online companies and monetize your traffic by having a percentage of sales generated by traffic coming from your site.

The basic idea is, traffic generated from your site will go to another site that can offer a product that you do not carry. Many programs can keep track and make records of transactions that was made possible because of site linkage.

When purchases are made by customers that was led by your site to their site you get a percentage of that sale. Affiliate programs would give you the benefit of monetizing your traffic without the actual need of carrying or promoting a certain product.

There are so many ways and methods to monetize your traffic. All it takes is a bit of hard work and the desire to successfully launch a profit-earning site. The internet is a veritable source of information, many tips and guides are offered everywhere in how to monetize your traffic and make your site a good profit earner.

How To Use A Tell A Friend Script To Drive Traffic Today

More and more webmasters have the recurring dilemma on how to increase the flow of traffic in the websites. During the past few years many methods that been developed to solve this predicament. While most of them would work there are those that would not make even a small impact.

One of the methods that have spawned many success stories in driving traffic into websites is viral marketing. Viral marketing makes use of the tendency of a person to share something to find informative, entertaining or amazing.

Many companies bank on this behavior to spread their products and increase the popularity of their company or their website. Viral marketing makes use of many mediums in enticing this behavior. It might be in the form of an interesting story, an addicting flash game, an amusing video and many others that may catch a person's fancy.

This ingenious form of marketing is typically low cost and is a wonderful tool for any company to utilize. The benefit greatly overshadows the cost or efforts to initialize this marketing scheme. Any website would greatly benefit that viral marketing.

Tell A Friend Script

One of the easiest methods in viral marketing is using a tell a friend script. This is a simple programming script that you can attach to the programming of your website. Generally, tell a friends script are installed in pages where a media is placed so that a person can easily send the media to any of his friends or his family members.

The basic concept of a tell a friend script is a script wherein a person may input his name, e-mail address, the recipient's e-mail address and send the media to the intended recipient much like an e-mail with an attachment. As the recipient receives the e-mail he wouldn't think of the mail a spam mail because he would see the sender's name as someone he or she knows and trust.

Tell a friend script eliminates greatly the chances of being blocked because they use the information inputted by the sender. This allows for wider spreading of this marketing method. It can be quite sneaky but it is very effective.

With the e-mail sent and opened the sent media will either be read, viewed or played. Also along with the mail would be a brief description of the company or site that sponsors the media sent. This allows for the introduction of either the site, company name or its products. The along with it is another tell a friend script.

Then the process begins again. As more people use the tell a friend script, more and more people will know of the existence of the sponsoring company or site. People who read the ads inside the mail who liked what they see would go and click on the link and visit the site. This drives traffic into the site resulting to great number of potential customers.

Tell A Friend Script Availability

A tell a friend script is very simple and does not require a complicated method of programming. In fact, you can copy paste a script and simply put it on an intended page. Finding one is even simpler. All you have to do is go to a search engine and type in the search box "tell a friend script" then press enter or click go.

In the search results page you will see many links that will direct you to a site where you can get a tell a friend script. It would just be a simple matter of looking and searching for the script and copying it to your intended web page.

With a tell a friend script viral marketing strategy you can drive traffic into your site which could potentially spell profits. This is a simple harmless script that offers great benefits for low cost paired with great creativity and foresight.

It is imperative that you have patience in using a tell a friend script. If your chosen media doesn't get the mileage that is expected of it, it may take some time before it gets spread or shared. But surely many people will see your ads and there is great probability that they will visit your site increasing your traffic flow.

7 Surefire Ways To Increase Your Traffic Starting Yesterday

Internet. Business. Profit. To fully integrate all of these words into a successful merging you will need another word. Traffic. Every article you will find about making your site or company successful would always include the importance of generating traffic.

So, we all know that in the core of it all, traffic is the most essential thing to a successful internet based business company. Aside from ensuring that you have a great product to sell, and you have your company's internal organization well taken core of, it would be time to get to the nitty gritty of things, generating traffic.

If you already have a site and you want think that you're not getting the traffic that you're supposed to be getting, then its time to reconsider. If you are contending in these very competitive business, you should always be a step ahead of your competition, increasing your traffic flow should have been done starting yesterday.

Timing is essential, that's an old adage known to everyone. But with generating traffic, you should always be on your toes and be a day ahead of everyone. Never think of today and tomorrow as a starting point for making your site traffic laden, it should always have been yesterday.

To help you out in generating more traffic for your site, here are some seven surefire ways to increase your traffic starting from yesterday.

1) Invest in good advertising with search engines

Google's Adwords and Yahoo's Overture provide great advertising schemes that are very truly popular and assures great traffic. Although with this surefire way to increase your traffic would cost some money. While some would shy away from spending money to increase traffic, it is imperative in this case to do so because Adwords and Overture is the top surefire way to increase your traffic.

You could see for yourself the success this search engine advertising methods have reaped rewards for so many companies. Lots of site feature these advertising system and many have signed on to reap the benefits. Do not be left behind. Every penny is worth it with using Google and Yahoo's advertising.

2) Exchange or Trade Links with other sites

With exchanging links with other sites, both of you will benefit from the efforts both of you do to enhance your sites traffic. When one site features another sites link, they could provide one another with the traffic one site generates. The efforts are doubly beneficial because it would seem like both of you are working to generate more traffic. The more links traded with more sites the more traffic could be expected.

3) Use Viral Marketing

Viral marketing allows you to spread the word about your company and product without any costs or if ever low costs only. This is a marketing method that can be quite sneaky; you can attach your company's name, product or link to a certain media such as a funny video, entertaining game, an interesting article or a gossip or buzz. With this method, people get infected with the creativity and entertainment of the medium that they will pass it on to many people.

4) Search and use proper keywords or keyword phrases for your sites content

Search engines look for certain keywords that they would show in their results page. In doing so, having the right keyword and keyword phrase is a high requirement in ranking in high in search engine results. You could write your own content or you could hire someone to do it for you.

5) Write Articles that can lead traffic to your site

Submit articles to sites that would contain the same subject that your site deals in. If you sell car parts write press releases and articles about cars and car parts. Attach your sites description and services at the end of the article as well as the link.

6) Join forums and form online communities

Capture a market and show your expertise and credibility. When you found a good foundation for your site, people will trust you and your site and will pass on to many people their trust. Traffic will certainly increase because they know that you can provide what they need.

7) Lastly, Offer newsletters.

If many people know what you are about and your existence is shared with many others, you will find a loyal traffic that can provide you with more traffic by recommendation. If you arouse the curiosity of your customers they would be pushed to help you with your traffic.

Search Engine Optimization And Why You Gotta Use It

E-commerce is a cut throat business. You have to arm yourself with the proper know-how and the tools to make your site a cut above the rest. Each day, more and more sites are clambering to optimize their rankings in websites and if you lose your guard, you may just get trampled on and be left in the abyss filled with so many failed e-commerce sites.

Search Engine Optimization or SEO is a term widely used today by many e-commerce sites. For the past few years and the next ten years or so, search engines would be the most widely used internet tool to find the sites that they need to go to or the product or information they need.

Most people that use search engines use only the ten top search results in the first page. Making it to the first page, more so to the top three is a barometer of a sites success in search engine optimization. You will get a higher ratio of probability in being clicked on when you rank high. The more traffic for your site, the more business you rake in.

But, it is essential to grab a hold of that spot or make your ranking even better. As I aforementioned, each day is a new day for all e-commerce sites to make them selves rank higher using search engine optimization. It is imperative to make your site better and better everyday.

So just what is search engine optimization and do you have to use it? The answer to why you have to use it is an easy one. You need search engine optimization to be number one, or maybe at least make your site income generating.

With search engine optimization you can get the benefit of generating a high traffic volume. Let's just say you get only a turn out of successful sales with 10 to 20 percent of your traffic. If you get a hundred hits or more a day, you get a good turn out of sales already. If you get only twenty to ten hits a day, you only get one or two if not any at all.

So once again, what is search engine optimization? Search engine optimization is utilizing tools and methods in making your site top ranking in the results of search engines. Getting yourself in the first page and better yet in the top half of the page will ensure that your site will generate public awareness of your site's existence and subsequently generate more traffic, traffic that could lead to potential income and business.

Search engine optimization requires a lot of work to be fully realized. There are many aspects you have to change in your site or add as well to get search engine optimization. These will include getting lots of information about the keyword phrases that are popular in regards to your sites niche or theme.

You may also need to rewrite your sites contents so that you could get the right keyword phrases in your site without making it too commercial but light and informative. There are certain rules and guidelines to be followed with making your site's content applicable and conducive to search engine optimization.

You will also need to collaborate with many other sites so that you could get link exchanges and page transfers. The more inbound and outbound traffics generated by sites among others are one of the components search engines uses to rank sites.

Try to search the internet for many useful help. Tips, guidelines and methods for search engine optimization are plenty to be found. Read many articles that can help you optimize your site in search engine results. The more knowledge and information you gather the better. This will all help you in getting those high rankings. This may require a little time and effort in your part but the benefits will be astounding.

If you can part with some money, there are many sites in the internet that can help you in search engine optimization. There are many sites that help in tracking keyword phrases that can help your site. There are also some content writers that have lots of experience in making good keyword laden content for your sites that have good quality.

Act now and see the benefits garner with search engine optimization. All of these will result to better traffic and more business for your site and company.

Top 5 Ways To Generate Low Cost Website Traffic

There is one hard and fast rule in generating income for your website: A steady flow of website traffic. If no one goes to your site, it hardly bares a chance of generating an income. Many sites have tried and failed in doing so, and these results to the sites demise. It takes money to maintain an income generating site; it also takes money to make money.

BUT, it doesn't take a whole caboodle of cash to generate website traffic for your site.

Ever wonder how does big hit sites drive traffic top their site? Most of them are spending tons of money to drive the traffic to their sites, investing in many advertising campaigns and different forms of marketing schemes and gimmickries. This is all worthwhile because, well, they are what they are now, high earning, big hitting websites.

You don't have to do this if you don't really have their resources. There are many ways to generate low cost website traffic without having to spend what you don't have or can't afford. Many people have banked on high cost methods and have ended up losing their shirt over it.

Here I present to you the Top five ways to generate low cost website traffic that could help your site a whole lot. Even if you only get a small percentage of successful visitors in to client ratio it still works especially if you get a high number of website traffic.

Exchange Links

This is a sure and proven method. Rarely would you see a site where there is no link to another site. Many webmasters are willing to exchange links with one another so that they could produce more public awareness about their sites. You'll soon see and feel the sudden upsurge of the traffic coming in to your site from other sites.

A major prerequisite in exchanging links with other sites is having the same niche or content as the other site. They should share a common subject so that there is continuity in the providing of service and information to what interests your target traffic.

Exchanging links also boosts your chances of getting a high ranking in search engine results. It is common knowledge that search engines ranks high sites that have inbound and outbound theme-related links. With a good ranking position in the search engines, you will generate more traffic in your website without the high costs.

Traffic Exchange

This is like exchanging links but on a different higher level. This may cost a bit more than exchanging or trading links but could be made cheaper because you get to earn credits. You can use those credits when viewing others traffic, while you earn credits when someone views yours.

Traffic exchange services are the viewing of another's site or page. This is done vice versa where a site can use your sites contents and so can you to his or her site. You both benefit from each others efforts to generate traffic. The other sites visitors can go to your pages and know more about your site as well as theirs. Once again the public awareness of your sites existence is boosted.

Write and Submit Articles

There are many e-zines and online encyclopedias in the internet which provides free space for articles to be submitted. If you want to save costs, you can do the articles yourself. There are many freelance writers who are willing to write for you for a small fee, but to save money, it is wise to do those articles yourself.

Write articles that are themed along with the niche of your site. Write something that you have expertise on so that when they read it, they can feel your knowledge about the subject and will be eager to go to your site. Write articles that produce tips and guidelines to the subject or niche your site has.

Include a resource box at the end of your article that can link them to your site. Write a little about yourself and your site. If you provide a light, information-laden and interesting article, they will go to your site for more.

Make a Newsletter.

This may sound like hard work because of all the articles you may need to use to build a newsletter but on the contrary, this is not so. There are many writers and sites that are willing to provide free articles as long as they can get their name in on your newsletter. This will also provide free advertising for them as well.

As your newsletter gets pass around, you can widen your public awareness and build an opt-in list that can regularly visit your site.

Join Online Communities and Forums

This only requires your time and nothing else. You can share your knowledge and expertise with many online communities as well as your website. You can get free advertising when you go to forums that have the same subject or niche with your site.

Share your two cents and let them see how knowledgeable you are with the subject. As you build your reputation, you also build the reputation of your site, making it a reputable and honest business that could be frequented and trusted by many people.

Using Google Adwords To Drive Laser Targeted Traffic

The biggest well known secret in generating wealth in the internet based business or e-commerce is Traffic. Everybody knows it; every site wants it and every site needs it. The point of websites is to be visited and viewed. Many elaborate designs, money and countless hours of developing a site to make them beautiful and attractive are utilized. Without traffic, it is for naught.

With traffic comes a potential customer which basically means sales which in turn means profit. While many sites have collapsed in the past with the downturn of many internet based business, many smaller sites have generated good money by concentrating on a certain niche and some subniches.

This is a reason why e-commerce site laser target certain groups of people and drive them to their site to showcase their sites and products. Precision marketing is essential so that you could count on all the traffic on your site as potential customers.

Using Money to Make Money

It's a common business notion that if you want to make money, you have to spend money. One good way of spending money for business gain is through advertising. Advertising brings in the people because through advertising, they know that there is such a company or product in existence. With the right type of advertising, you can see the spurt of traffic growth to your site. With a high volume of traffic, even if only a small portion or percentage turns out to be buying customers it is still a good average of profit generating income.

Right now, there is no other advertising scheme that would be worth every cent than using Google's Adwords. The surge in popularity of Google's Adwords is very evident as you can see so many sites sporting this ad scheme.

In using Google's Adwords, you pay a certain fee depending on the number of keywords your ad is keyword sensitive to. Each time a person does a search in Google, the keyword or keywords use generate ads in the side of Google which are generated by the keywords they have assigned for their ads.

This method laser targets the traffic a site wants for their site. This also ensures that you are readily visible in the first page of a search result. Paying Google for this ad scheme ensures that your target group of people sees your ads. You drive your laser targeted traffic to your site which provides for their needs and wants. You can also be sure that you can meet their demands and needs.

Aside from Google, you can also be featured in their other search networks, these includes sites like, AskJeeves, AOL Search and Netscape. These sites also show Adwords ads that react to searches done by visitors. There are also content networks, non-search engine sites that feature Google Adwords, which will also carry your ads. But this is subjected to the niche the site features. Your chosen keywords will determine which content network shall feature your ad. The frequency of your ad shall also be determined by your allowed budget.

Laser Targeting your Traffic

To get a good number or estimate of the traffic to buying customer ratio it is good to laser target your traffic. Knowing that your traffic are all potential customers and are interested in your products and company provides you with a more accurate statistics. This will show you how effective your utilizing of Google Adwords is.

Drive laser targeted traffic to your site by using keywords or keyword phrases for your Goggle Adwords that pertains to your company and to your products. There are many online internet tools that can help you in choosing keywords and keyword phrases that are currently in demand that could help drive laser targeted traffic to your site.

With your Google Adwords ad, you are ensured that every click to your ad is a potential customer that is precisely looking pr interested in what you have to offer. Make sure that your Google Adwords ad has the right keywords so that you can drive you're laser targeted traffic to your site.

Using Google Adwords to help boost the drive to increase laser targeted traffic will prove to be very beneficial as many other companies can attest to. The benefits are high with the cost relatively justifiable.

Viral Marketing 101 - Not Using It Could Kill Your Business!

Creativity.

This is one virtue a site must possess to lead the race in the ruthless competition in the Internet based business. With so many competition and rivalry going on, every method of marketing must be employed and utilized.

It doesn't matter if you have a killer product or a fantastically designed website, if people don't know that you exist, it doesn't matter, and you are not going to make it big. Worse of all, you business could just get killed.

While there are so many methods and schemes used by so many e-commerce sites today, there are still some of those that can help you with an extra boost in the popularity ratings. One of these is the so called Viral Marketing.

While the term Viral easily depicts a virus, a word very much dreaded by all computer owners, it is not what it seems. You do not actually use a computer virus to spread your business; on the contrary it just might kill you. Everyone has had enough of all those pop up ads and spywares.

Viral Marketing Overview

Viral Marketing also known otherwise as Viral Advertising is a marketing technique used to build the public awareness of one's product or company. They use many forms of media to reach out to the public without actually promoting the product by riding on in other forms of addictive means that could get a person hooked and be obliged or amused to actually pass it on, with the product or company advertisement along with it.

In a nutshell, companies ride on the idea that if people like the content of a media they will pass it on to their friends and family. They sponsor the certain media, such as a cool flash game, funny video, amusing story and such, which one may pass on to another with the company brand or logo or the products description or any other content to help promote the company or its product.

Viral marketing has become a popular means of advertising and marketing because they are relatively low cost. To avoid being tagged as spam mail, viral marketing counts on the eagerness of one person to pas on the product. If a person sees the name of the person they know as the sender, they won't block it and open it as well.

Many companies offer incentives such as discounts and rebates when they help in spreading their viral marketing. They rely on the number of recipients a viral marketing gets from one person in determining the amount or number of incentive they can be attributed with.

Using Viral Marketing to your advantage

The main and foremost advantage of viral marketing is that you get a lot of publicity and public awareness about your site and your company. You get to generate a flow of traffic that are potential customers. With a little ingenuity and imagination, plus some incentives or prizes, you can reach out to a great number of people and announce your existence.

Most every site and companies are catching on to the effectivity of Viral Marketing and Advertising. Not using it could kill your business. Along with other schemes and methods in promoting your site, like Search Engine Optimization and such, viral marketing could easily push you ahead in the rating games.

Viral Marketing could be a sneaky way to get people to know about you and your company. You get them to pass your advertisement along. They are also very low cost that not investing in it could be downright a business suicide. All it takes is a great idea, a good addicting game, a funny story many ideas are still out there. Create a gossip or a buzz, many movies are promoted by using scandals and gossips to make them moiré popular. Remember the movie "The Blair Witch Project"?

Many big companies have tried viral marketing and have had many success stories with it. A classic example is Microsoft's Hotmail. They were the first known big company to utilize the scheme and it has worked wonders for them.

Now it's your turn to use viral marketing to work wonders for you. Act now and reap the benefits Viral Marketing will provide for you and your sales figures.

Affiliate Marketing

3 Things All Affiliate Marketers Need To Survive Online

Every affiliate marketer is always looking for the successful market that gives the biggest paycheck. Sometimes they think it is a magic formula that is readily available for them. Actually, it is more complicated than that. It is just good marketing practices that have been proven over years of hard work and dedication.

There are tactics that have worked before with online marketing and is continuing to work in the online affiliate marketing world of today. With these top three marketing tips, you will be able to able to increase your sales and survive in the affiliate marketing online.

What are these three tactics?

1. Using unique web pages to promote each separate product you are marketing. Do not lump all of it together just to save some money on web hosting. It is best to have a site focusing on each and every product and nothing more.

Always include product reviews on the website so visitors will have an initial understanding on what the product can do to those who buys them. Also include testimonials from users who have already tried the product. Be sure that these customers are more than willing to allow you to use their names and photos on the site of the specific product you are marketing.

You can also write articles highlighting the uses of the product and include them on the website as an additional page. Make the pages attractive compelling and include calls to act on the information. Each headline should attract the readers to try and read more, even contact you. Highlight your special points. This will help your readers to learn what the page is about and will want to find out more.

2. Offer free reports to your readers. If possible position them at the very top side of your page so it they simply cannot be missed. Try to create autoresponder messages that will be mailed to those who input their personal information into your sign up box. According to research, a sale is closed usually on the seventh contact with a prospect.

Only two things can possibly happen with the web page alone: closed sale or the prospect leaving the page and never return again. By placing useful information into their inboxes at certain specified period, you will remind them of the product they thought they want later and will find out that the sale is closed. Be sure that the content is directed toward specific reasons to buy the product. Do not make it sound like a sales pitch.

Focus on important points like how your product can make life and things easier and more enjoyable. Include compelling subject lines in the email. As much as possible, avoid using the word "free" because there are still older spam filters that dumps those kind of contents into the junk before even anyone reading them first. Convince those who signed up for your free reports that they will be missing something big if they do not avail of your products and services.

3. Get the kind of traffic that is targeted to your product. Just think, if the person who visited your website has no interest whatsoever in what you are offering, they will be among those who move on and never come back. Write articles for publication in e-zines and e-reports. This way you can locate publications that is focusing on your target customers and what you have put up might just grab their interest.

Try to write a minimum of 2 articles per week, with at least 300-600 words in length. By continuously writing and maintaining these articles you can generate as many as 100 targeted readers to your site in a day.

Always remember that only 1 out of 100 people are likely to buy your product or get your services. If you can generate as much as 1,000 targeted hits for your website in a day, that means you can made 10 sales based on the average statistic.

The tactics given above does not really sound very difficult to do, if you think about it. It just requires a little time and an action plan on your part.

Try to use these tips for several affiliate marketing programs. You can end maintaining a good source of income and surviving in this business that not all marketers can do.

Besides, think of the huge paychecks you will be receiving…

A Day In The Life Of An Affiliate Marketer

Being in the affiliate marketing business is not that hard now with the internet at your disposable. It is much easier now compared to the days when people have to make use of the telephones and other mediums of information just to get the latest updates on the way their program is coming along.

So with technology at hand, and assuming that the affiliate is working from home, a day in his or her life would sound something like this…

Upon waking up and after having breakfast, the computer is turned on to check out new developments in the network. As far as the marketer is concerned there might be new things to update and statistics to keep track on.

The site design has to be revised. The marketer knows that a well-designed site can increase sign ups from visitors. It can also help in the affiliate's conversion rates.

That done, it is time to submit the affiliate program to directories that lists affiliate programs. These directories are means to attract people in joining your affiliate program. A sure way of promoting the affiliate program.

Time to track down the sales you are getting from your affiliates fairly and accurately. There are phone orders and mails to track down. See if they are new clients checking the products out. Noting down the contact information that might be a viable source in the future.

There are lots of resources to sort out. Ads, banners, button ads and sample recommendations to give out because the marketer knows that this is one way of ensuring more sales. Best to stay visible and accessible too.

The affiliate marketer remembered that there are questions to answer from the visitors. This has to be done quickly. Nothing can turn off a customer than an unanswered email.

To prove that the affiliate is working effectively and efficiently, inquiries would have to be paid more attention on. Nobody wants to be ignored and customers are not always the most patient of all people. Quick answer that should appear professional yet friendly too.

In the process of doing all the necessities, the marketer is logged on to a chat room where he or she interacts with other affiliates and those under that same program. This is where they can discuss things on how to best promote their products.

There are things to be learned and it is a continuous process. Sharing tips and advices is a good way of showing support. There may be others out there wanting to join and may be enticed by the discussion that is going on. There is no harm in assuming what opportunities ahead.

The newsletters and ezines were updated days ago, so it is time for the affiliate marketer to see if there are some new things happening in the market. This will be written about in the marketer's publication to be distributed to the old and new customers.

These same publications are also an important tool in keeping up to date with the newly introduced products. The marketer has put up a sale and promotion that customers may want to know about. Besides, they have to keep up with the deadline of these sales written in the publications.

It is that time to show some appreciation to those who have helped the marketer in the promotions and sale increase. Nothing like mentioning the persons, their sites and the process they have done that made everything worked.

Of course, this will be published in the newsletters. Among the more important information that have been written already.

The marketer still has time to write out recommendations to those who want credible sources for the products being promoted. There is also time to post some comments on how to be a successful affiliate marketer on a site where there are lots of wannabees.

Two objectives done at the same time. The marketer gets to promote the product as well as the program they are in. Who knows, someone may be inclined to join.

Time flies. Missed lunch but is quite contented with the tasks done. Bed time….

Ok, so this may not be all done in a day. But then, this gives you an idea of how an affiliate marketer, a dedicated one that is, spends the marketing day.

Is that success looming in the distance or what?

Easy Profits Using PPC In Your Affiliate Marketing Business

PPC is one of the four basic types of Search Engines. PPC is also one of the most cost-effective ways of targeted internet advertising. According to Forbes magazine, PPC or Pay Per Click, accounts to 2 billion dollars a year and is expected to increase to around 8 billion dollars by the year 2008.

Let us take a quick look at how PPC Search Engines work.

These engines create listings and rate them based on a bid amount the website owner is willing to pay for each click from that search engine. Advertisers bid against each other to receive higher ranking for a specific keyword or phrase.

The highest bidder for a certain keyword or phrase will then have the site ranked as number 1 in the PPC Search Engines followed by the second and third highest bidder, up to the last number that have placed a bid on the same keyword or phrase. Your ads then will appear prominently on the results pages based on the dollar amount bid you will agree to pay per click.

How do you make money by using PPC into your affiliate marketing business?

Most affiliate programs only pay when a sale is made or a lead delivered after a visitor has clickthrough your site. Your earnings will not always be the same as they will be dependent on the web site content and the traffic market.

The reason why you should incorporate PPC into your affiliate marketing program is that earnings are easier to make than in any other kind of affiliate program not using PPC. This way, you will be making profit based from the clickthroughs that your visitor will make on the advertiser's site. Unlike some programs, you are not paid per sale or action.

PPC can be very resourceful of your website. With PPC Search Engines incorporated into your affiliate program, you will be able to profit from the visitor's who are not interested in your products or services. The same ones who leave your site and never comes back.

You will not only get commissions not only from those who are just searching the web and finding the products and services that they wanted but you will be able to build your site's recognition as a valuable resource. The visitors who have found what they needed from you site are likely to come back and review what you are offering more closely. Then they will eventually come back to search the web for other products.

This kind of affiliate program is also an easy way for you to generate some more additional revenues. For example, when a visitor on your site does a search in the PPC Search Engine and clicks on the advertiser bided listings, the advertisers' account will then be deducted because of that click. With this, you will be compensated 30% to 80% of the advertisers' bid amount.

PPC is not only a source of generating easy profits; it can also help you promote your own site. Most of the programs allow the commissions received to be spent for advertising with them instantly and with no minimum earning requirement. This is one of the more effective ways to exchange your raw visitors for targeted surfers who has more tendencies to purchase your products and services.

What will happen if you when you integrate PPC into your affiliate program?

PPC usually have ready-to-use affiliate tools that can be easily integrated into your website. The most common tools are search boxes, banners, text links and some 404-error pages. Most search engines utilize custom solutions and can provide you with a white-label affiliate program. This enables you, using only a few lines of code, to integrate remotely-hosted co-branded search engine into your website.

The key benefits? Not only more money generated but also some extra money on the side. Plus a lifetime commissions once you have referred some webmaster friends to the engine.

Think about it. Where can you get all these benefits while already generating some income for your site? Knowing some of the more useful tools you can use for your affiliate program is not a waste of time. They are rather a means of earning within an earning.

Best know more about how you can use PPC search engines into your affiliate program than miss out on a great opportunity to earn more profits.

Here's How To Avoid The 3 Most Common Affiliate Mistakes

Affiliate marketing is one of the most effective and powerful ways of earning some money online. This program gives everybody a chance to make a profit through the Internet. Since these affiliate marketing programs are easy to join, implement and pays a commission on a regular basis, more an more people are now willing in this business.

However, like all businesses, there are lots of pitfalls in the affiliate marketing business. Committing some of the most common mistakes will cost the marketers a large portion taken from the profit they are making everyday. That is why it is better to avoid them than be regretful in the end.

Mistake number 1: Choosing the wrong affiliate.

Many people want to earn from affiliate marketing as fast as possible. In their rush to be part of one, they tend to choose a bandwagon product. This is the kind of products that the program thinks is "hot". They choose the product that is in demand without actually considering if the product appeals to them. This is not a very wise move obviously.

Instead of jumping on the bandwagon, try top choose a product in which you are truly interested in. For any endeavor to succeed, you should take some time to plan and figure out your actions.

Pick a product that appeals to you. Then do some research about that product to see if they are in demand. Promoting a product you are more passionate about is easier than promoting one for the sake of the earnings only.

Mistake number 2: Joining too many affiliate programs.

Since affiliate programs are very easy to join, you might be tempted to join multiples of affiliate programs to try and maximize the earnings you will be getting. Besides you may think that there is nothing wrong and nothing to lose by being part of many affiliate programs.

True, that is a great way to have multiple sources of income. However, joining multiple programs and attempting to promote them all at the same time will prevent you from concentrating on each one of them.

The result? The maximum potential of your affiliate program is not realized and the income generated will not exactly be as huge as you were thinking initially it would. The best way to get excellent result is by joining just one program that pays a 40% commission at least. Then give it your best effort by promoting your products enthusiastically. As soon as you see that it is already making a reasonable profit, then maybe you can now join another affiliate program.

The technique is to do it slowly but surely. There is really no need to rush into things, especially with affiliate marketing. With the way things are going, the future is looking real bright and it seems affiliate marketing will be staying for a long time too.

Mistake number 3: Not buying the product or using the service.

As an affiliate, you main purpose is to effectively and convincingly promote a product or service and to find customers. For you to achieve this purpose, you must be able to relay to the customers that certain product and service. It is therefore difficult for you to do this when you yourself have not tried these things out. Thus, you will fail to promote and recommend them convincingly. You will also fail to create a desire in your customers to avail any of what you are offering.

Try the product or service personally first before you sign up as an affiliate to see if it is really delivering what it promises. If you have done so, then you are one of the credible and living testaments aware of its advantages and disadvantages. Your customers will then feel the sincerity and truthfulness in you and this will trigger them to try them out for themselves.

Many affiliate marketers makes these mistakes and are paying dearly for their actions. To not fall into the same situation they have been in, try to do everything to avoid making the same mistakes.

Time is the key. Take the time to analyze your marketing strategy and check if youa re in the right track. If done properly, you will be able to maximize your affiliate marketing program and earn higher profits.

Here's Why Using Camtasia Can Increase Your Affiliate Checks

Since there are already lots of people getting into affiliate marketing, it is no wonder that the competition is getting stiff. The challenge is to try and outdo other affiliates and think of ways to be able to attain this.

There are also many tips and techniques being taught to these affiliate in order to best plan their strategy for their program to work effectively so that more earnings will be achieved.

What better way to wow your prospects and customers than to record and publish top notch, full motion and streaming screen-captured videos. Nothing like feeling your hard work getting paid by having your customers jumping up excitedly in great anticipation to buy your product right there and then.

This is Camtasia in action. It is a proven fact; giving your customers something they can actually see can explode your online sales instantly.

You do not need to have trainings and education to be able to know how this system can work for your affiliate program. Anyone can create stunning videos, from multimedia tutorials and step-by-step presentations available online. The process is like having your customers seated next to you and looking at your desktop, as you show them the things they need to see and hear. All this done step by step.

For those who does not know it yet, how does Camtasia works?

1. It can record your desktop activity in a single click. No need to have to save and compile all your files because it is recorded right there and then.

2. Can easily convert your videos into web pages. Once converted you can have your customers visiting that certain page. Videos are easier to understand and take in unlike reading texts which oftentimes is a trying thing to do.

3. Upload your pages. Publish them through blogs, RSS feed and podcasts. You may want your Camtasis videos to get around and reach out to other people that may be potential customers in the future. Nothing like being visible in many sites and pages to advertise yourself and get your message through.

There are other things you can do with your affiliate program using Camtasia. You can...

Create stunning multimedia presentations that are proven to increase sales because all the senses are engaged. This also has the tendency to reduce skepticism among hard-to-please customers.

Reduce refunds and other customer issues by demonstrating visually how to use your product and how to do it properly. Complaints will also be minimized because all the facts and the presentation are there for the customers to just see and hear about.

Promote affiliate products and services using visual presentations. This is an effective way of redirecting your viewers straight to your affiliate website after they are finished with the video. Make the most of the presentation by putting your site location in the end and make them go there directly if they want more information.

Multiple your online auction bids exponentially when you give your readers a feel of what you have to offer. Based from reports, auctions that includes pictures increases bidding percentage by 400%. Imagine how much higher it will be if it were videos.

Publish valuable infoproducts that you can sell for a much higher price. It will be all worth the price because of the full colored graphics menu and templates that you will be using.

Minimize miscommunication with your customers. Instantly showing them what you want they wanted in the first place is making them understand clearly the essence of your affiliate program. The good thing about multimedia is, nothing much can go wrong. It is there already.

These are just some of the things you can do with Camtasia that can be very helpful in your chosen affiliate program.

Note that the main purpose of using Camtasia is to boost the income that is generated from your affiliate program. Although it can be used for entertainment and enjoyment purposes, which is not really a valid reason why you choose to get all through that trouble.

Try to focus on the goal that you have set upon yourself to and achieve that with the use of the things that may be quite a lot of help in increasing your earnings.

How To Become A Super Affiliate In Niche Markets

Over the past years, web hosting has grown bigger than it used to be. With more companies getting into this business and finding the many benefits it can give them, the demand for web hosting has never been higher. These seem to be the trend of today.

38 million people have put up their very first websites online this year 2005 alone. It is estimated that by 2008, the internet sales industry will top then dollar bank. And to think, majority of those sites will be offering different affiliate programs for people to choose and participate into.

This only means one thing. It is easier now to find the right web host for your application. The possibility of quality web hosting companies separating themselves from the rest of the industry is anticipated. If this is done, the unprofessional and incompetent ones will suffer.

Support will be the number one consideration for people when choosing a web host. It will be obvious that traditional advertising will become less and less effective. Most people would rather opt for the web host based on things that they see and hear. Also based on the recommendations by those who have tried them and have proved to be a successful.

This is a great opportunity for web hosting affiliates and resellers alike. There would hundreds of web hosting and programs to choose from that the difficulty in finding the right one for them is not a problem anymore.

How does one become a successful affiliate in the niche markets using web hosting?

If you think about it, everyone who needs a website needs a web hosting company to host it for them. As of now, there is really no leading hosting industry so most people choose hosts based from recommendations. Usually, they get it from the ones that have already availed of a web hosting services.

With the many hosts offering affiliate programs, there is the tendency to find the one which you think will work best for you. Think of the product you will be promoting. Pattern them to the site and see if they are catering to the same things as you are.

When you have been with one host for quite some time and seem not to be making much despite all your effort, leave that one and look for another. There is no use in trying to stick to one when you would be before off in another one. Things will only have to get better from there because you already have been in worst situations.

Try this out. If you are quite happy and satisfied with your web host, try to see if they are offering an affiliate program you can participate on. Instead of you paying them, why not make it the other way around; them paying you. The process can be as easy as putting a small "powered by" or "hosted by" link at the bottom of your page and you are already in an affiliate business.

Why choose paying for your for your web hosting when you do not have to? Try to get paid by letting people know you like your web host.

Always remember that when choosing a web host, choose the one that is known for its fantastic customer support. There are also many hosting affiliate programs. Residual affiliate program is also being hosted. This is the program wherein you get paid a percentage every month for a client that you refer. This can allow you to have a steady source of income. With perseverance, you can even be quite successful in this field.

There are a lot of niche markets out there just waiting for the right affiliate to penetrate to them and make that dollars dream come true. Knowing which one to get into is being confident enough of your potentials and the good results you will be getting.

Web hosting is just one affiliate market you could try out and make some good and continuous income. Just remember that to be successful on your endeavor also means that time, effort and patience is needed.

Nobody has invented the perfect affiliate market yet. But some people do know how to make it big in this kind of market. It is just knowing your kind of market and making the earnings there.

So Many Affiliate Programs! Which One Do I Choose?

Ask questions first before you join an affiliate program. Do a little research about the choices of program that you intend to join into. Get some answers because they will be the deciding point of what you will be achieving later on.

Will it cost you anything to join? Most affiliate programs being offered today are absolutely free of charge. So why settle for those that charge you some dollars before joining.

When do they issue the commission checks? Every program is different. Some issue their checks once a month, every quarter, etc. Select the one that is suited to your payment time choice. Many affiliate programs are setting a minimum earned commission amount that an affiliate must meet or exceed in order for their checks to be issued.

What is the hit per sale ratio? This is the average number of hits to a banner or text link it takes to generate a sale based on all affiliate statistics. This factor is extremely important because this will tell you how much traffic you must generate before you can earn a commission from the sale.

How are referrals from an affiliate's site tracked and for how long do they remain in the system? You need to be confident on the program enough to track those people you refer from your site. This is the only way that you can credit for a sale. The period of time that those people stay in the system is also important. This is because some visitors do not buy initially but may want to return later to make the purchase. Know if you will still get credit for the sale if it is done some months from a certain day.

What are the kinds of affiliate stats available? Your choice of affiliate program should be capable of offering detailed stats. They should be available online anytime you decide to check them out. Constantly checking your individual stats is important to know how many impressions, hits and sales are already generated from your site. Impressions are the number of times the banner or text link was viewed by a visitor of your site. A hit is the one clicking on the banner or text links.

Does the affiliate program also pay for the hits and impressions besides the commissions on sales? It is important that impressions and hits are also paid, as this will add to the earnings you get from the sales commission. This is especially important if the program you are in offers low sales to be able to hit ratio.

Who is the online retailer? Find out whom you are doing business with to know if it is really a solid company. Know the products they are selling and the average amount they are achieving. The more you know about the retailer offering you the affiliate program, the easier it will be for you to know if that program is really for you and your site.

Is the affiliate a one tier or two tier program? A single tier program pays you only for the business you yourself have generated. A two tier program pays you for the business, plus it also pays you a commission on the on the sales generated by any affiliate you sponsor in your program. Some two-tier programs are even paying small fees on each new affiliate you sponsor. More like a recruitment fee.

Lastly, what is the amount of commission paid? 5% - 20% is the commission paid by most programs. .01% - .05% is the amount paid for each hit. If you find a program that also pays for impressions, the amount paid is not much at all. As you can see from the figures, you will now understand why the average sales amount and hit to sale ratio is important.

These are just some of the questions that needed answering first before you enter into an affiliate program. You should be familiar with the many important aspects that your chosen program should have before incorporating them into your website. Try to ask your affiliate program choices these questions. These can help you select the right program for you site from among the many available.

Top 3 Ways To Boost Your Affiliate Commissions Overnight

The ideal world of affiliate marketing does not require having your won website, dealing with customers, refunds, product development and maintenance. This is one of the easiest ways of launching into an online business and earning more profits.

Assuming you are already into an affiliate program, what would be the next thing you would want to do? Double, or even triple, your commissions, right? How do you do that?

Here are some powerful tips on how to boost your affiliate program commissions overnight.

1. Know the best program and products to promote. Obviously, you would want to promote a program that will enable you to achieve the greatest profits in the shortest possible time.

There are several factors to consider in selecting such a program. Choose the ones that have a generous commission structure. Have products that fit in with your target audience. And that has a solid track record of paying their affiliate easily and on time. If you cannot seem to increase your investments, dump that program and keep looking for better ones.

There are thousands of affiliate programs online which gives you the reason to be picky. You may want to select the best to avoid losing your advertising dollars.

Write free reports or short ebooks to distribute from your site. There is a great possibility that you are competing with other affiliates that are promoting the same program. If you start writing short report related to the product you are promoting, you will be able to distinguish yourself from the other affiliates.

In the reports, provide some valuable information for free. If possible, add some recommendations about the products. With ebooks, you get credibility. Customers will see that in you and they will be enticed to try out what you are offering.

2. Collect and save the email addresses of those who download your free ebooks. It is a known fact that people do not make a purchase on the first solicitation. You may want to send out your message more than six times to make a sale.

This is the simple reason why you should collect the contact information of those who downloaded your reports and ebooks. You can make follow-ups on these contacts to remind them to make a purchase from you.

Get the contact information of a prospect before sending them to the vendor's website. Keep in mind that you are providing free advertisement for the product owners. You get paid only when you make a sale. If you send prospects directly to the vendors, chances are they would be lost to you forever.

But when you get their names, you can always send other marketing messages to them to be able to earn an ongoing commission instead of a one-time sale only.

Publish an online newsletter or Ezine. It is always best to recommend a product to someone you know than to sell to a stranger. This is the purpose behind publishing your own newsletter. This also allows you to develop a relationship based on trust with your subscribers.

This strategy is a delicate balance between providing useful information with a sales pitch. If you continue to write informative editorials you will be able to build a sense of reciprocity in your readers that may lead them to support you by buying your products.

3. Ask for higher than normal commission from merchants. If you are already successful with a particular promotion, you should try and approach the merchant and negotiate a percentage commission for your sales.

If the merchant is smart, he or she will likely grant your request rather than lose a valuable asset in you. Keep in mind that you are a zero-risk investment to your merchant; so do not be shy about requesting for addition in your commissions. Just try to be reasonable about it.

Using Product Recommendations To Increase Your Bottom Line

In affiliate marketing, there are many ways in which you can increase your earnings and maintain the account that you have worked so hard for already. Most of the techniques and tactics can be learned easily. No need to go anywhere and any further. They are available online, 24 hours a day and 7 days a week.

One of the more important ways of increasing affiliate marketing bottom line and sale is through the use of product recommendations. Many marketers know that this is one of the most effective ways in promoting a certain product.

If the customers or visitors trust you enough, then they will definitely trust your recommendations. Be very careful in using this approach, though. If you start promoting everything by recommendation, your credibility will actually wear thin. This is seen especially when recommendations are seemingly exaggerated and without much merit.

Do not be afraid to mention things that you do not like about a given product or service. Rather than lose any points for you, this will make your recommendation more realistic and will tend to increase your credibility.

Furthermore, if your visitors are really interested in what you are offering, they will be more than delighted to learn what is good about the product, what is not so good, and how the product will benefit them.

When you are recommending a certain product, there are some things to remember on how to make it work effectively and for your advantage.

Sound like the true and leading expert in your field.

Remember this simple equation: Price resistance diminishes in direct proportion to trust. If your visitors feel and believe that you are an expert in your niche, they are more inclined to making that purchase. On the other hand, if you are not exuding any confidence and self-assurance in endorsing your products, they will probably feel that same way and will go in search of another product or service which is more believable.

How do you establish this aura of expertise? By offering unique and new solutions they would not get anywhere else. Show proof that what you are promoting works as promised. Display prominent testimonials and endorsements from respected and known personalities, in related fields of course.

Avoid hype at all costs. It is better to sound low key and confident, than to scream and seek attention. Besides, you would not want to sound unprofessional and have that thinking stick to your potential customers and clients, now would you? Best to appear cool and self-assured at the same time.

And remember; prospects are not stupid. They are actually turning to experts and may already know the things that you know. If you back up your claims with hard facts and data, they would gladly put down hundreds, or even thousands worth of money to your promotions. But if you don't, they are smart enough to try and look at your competitors and what they are offering.

While recommending a product, it is also important that you give out promotional freebies. People are already familiar with the concept of offering freebies to promoting your won products. But very few people do this to promote affiliate products. Try to offer freebies that can promote or even have some information about your products or services.

Before you add recommendations to you product, it is given that you should try and test the product and support. Do not run the risk of promoting junk products and services. Just think how long it took you to build credibility and trust among your visitors. All that will take to destroy it is one big mistake on your part.

If possible, have recommendations of products that you have 100% confidence in. Test the product support before you begin to ensure that the people you are referring it to would not be left high and dry when a problem suddenly arouse.

Have a look at your affiliate market and look at the strategies you are using. You may not be focusing on the recommendations that your products need to have. You plan of action is sometimes not the only thing that is making your program works.

Try product recommendation and be among those few who have proven its worth.

Which Affiliate Networks To Look Out For When Promoting

There are many horror stories about affiliate programs and networks. People have heard them over and over again, that some are even wary of joining one. The stories they may have heard are those related to illegal programs or pyramid schemes. Basically, this kind of market does not have real, worthy product.

You do not want to be associated with these schemes. It is obvious you want to be with a program that offers high quality product that you will readily endorse. The growing number of those who have joined already and are succeeding immensely is proof enough that there are reliable and quality affiliate programs out there.

Why participate in an affiliate program?

It allows you to work part-time. It gives you the opportunity to build a generous residual income. And it makes you an owner of a small business. Affiliate programs have already created lots of millionaires. They are the living testimony of how hard work; continuous prospecting, motivating and training others pay off.

If ever you are deciding to join one, you must take note that you are getting into something that is patterned to what you are capable of. This will be an assurance that you are capable of doing anything to come out successful.

How do you choose a good affiliate program to promote? Here are some tips you may want to look over before choosing one:

1. A program that you like and have interest in. One of the best ways of knowing if that is the kind of program you wish to promote is if you are interested in purchasing the product yourself. If that is the case, chances are, there are many others who are also interested in the same program and products.

2. Look for a program that is of high quality. For instance, look for one that is associated with many experts in that particular industry. This way, you are assured that of the standard of the program you will be joining into.

3. Join in the ones that offer real and viable products. How do you know this? Do some initial research. If possible, track down some of the members and customers to give you testimonial on the credibility of the program.

4. The program that is catering to a growing target market. This will ensure you that there will be more and continuous demands for your referrals. Make inquiries. There are forums and discussions you can participate in to get good and reliable feedbacks.

5. A program with a compensation plan that pays out a residual income and a payout of 30% or more would be a great choice. There are some programs offering this kind of compensation. Look closely for one. Do not waste your time with programs that do not reward substantially for your efforts.

6. Be aware of the minimum quotas that you must fulfill or sales target that is too hard to achieve. Some affiliate programs imposes pre-requisites before you get your commissions. Just be sure that you are capable of attaining their requirements.

7. Select one that has plenty of tools and resources that can help you grow the business in the shortest possible time. Not all affiliate programs have these capacities. Make use you decide on one with lots of helpful tools you can use.

8. Check out if the program has a proven system that can allow you to check your networks and compensation. Also check if they have it available online for you to check anytime and anywhere.

9. The program that is offering strong incentives for members to renew their membership each time. The affiliate program that provides continuous help and upgrades for its products have the tendency to retain its members. These things can assure the growth of your networks.

10. Be aware of the things that members are not happy about in a program. Like with the ones mentioned above, you can do your checking at discussion forums. If you know someone in that same program, there is ho harm asking if there are many downsides involved.

Article Marketing

3 Things You Must Do Before You Submit To Article Directories

To all writers and non-writers out there, now is the time to start digging up those creative writing skills back.

With modern communication technology comes the popularity of information-based marketing, which is one of the oldest and most effective techniques in getting targeted prospects to sites and converting them into buyers. This is why article writing, submissions and publications are also getting popular.

There are already many tools that people can use to make the process of distributing their articles more easily. Though this is invaluable in getting the contents more exposure, which is only half of the story.

Let us take a look first at the common mistakes that some people make before submitting their contents to article directories:

1. Confusing the reason to promote the articles with the reason to write them.

In article writing, there are three key benefits why you are promoting them; branding, lead generation and promotion, which are all part of your optimization efforts.

But there is only one reason why you write an article, and that is to inform your audience. If the article is not focused on this primary and most important purpose, it will fail to achieve the three promotion benefits because no one will be interested in reading them.

You need to figure out first how to get people to read what is in your article, then make them click on your resource box. You can achieve this by producing better contents.

2. Failing to maximize the promotional opportunities of article marketing.

You may know already that your articles can help you generate additional links back to your site. But do you know that you can get more visitors and better search engine results from that same articles?

Mention keywords at strategic places. Just be sure not to overdo them. Some are even using anchor texts which is also an effective method. But it is important to know that majority of the directories are not able to support this.

Remember that is not only about the links back to your site. Part of doing well in your article marketing is getting picked up by publishers with a large number of audiences and gaining the ability of leveraging other brands because of the quality of your work. Better search engine results also are great benefits.

But these things do not put much money in your pocket. There are other factors that can turn your article marketing efforts into an opportunity that can boost your earnings. Not just increase the number of visitors to your site.

Start out with a plan and see to it that your article will serve the function that you intended it to have.

3. Publishing content that does not help your readers.

Maybe in the process of writing articles, you are thinking that all that is you wanted is links back to your site. And any visitors it can generate are fine.

Guess what? Not all article banks and directories are going to accept your content automatically. Oftentimes, they have some guidelines and specifications on the articles that they are accepting.

You can double the number of sites you can submit to by writing articles that the directories want to share with other people. All it takes is one publisher with a hundred thousand readers to increase your potential audience overnight.

Write the articles that publishers want in their publications if you want your article marketing to work the most effective way for you. This also means you have to obey the standard guidelines, spell checks, researching on a good topic and even hiring a writer to produce a good content on your behalf.

In the end, it is all really a matter of choice on your part. You can start getting a little exposure from increased links back but on a very basic level. Or enjoy massive exposure from a little extra time making quality contents.

It will be your choice. You may not be aware of the fact that an article submitted on directories is not meant to have the same level of exposure as highly-targeted content ones geared on a narrow group of people.

Learn the difference between these two and it will surely help you know what kinds of articles to write and to submit.

4 Things ALL Articles Must Have - Don't Forget!

The importance of articles in today's websites and internet based companies are immeasurable. They dictate a lot in the success and the drive of traffic into one's site. It has become a key element in making a site work and earns a profit. A website operator and owner must have the good sense to include articles in his or her site that will work for them and earn them the many benefits articles can give to their site.

Articles have been known to be the driving force in driving traffic to a website. Articles are a factor in giving site high rankings in search result pages. The higher a site ranks the bigger slice of the traffic flow pie he gets. With a huge number in traffic flow, there are more profits and more potential for other income generating schemes as well.

But, it is not just about stuffing your site with articles; they have certain requirements as well. These requirements must be met to obtain the maximum benefits an article will provide for your site. A well written article will catch the eyes and interest of your customers and keep them coming back for more. They would also be able to recommend your site to others.

Here are some tips to help you and assist you in making your articles. Below you will read about four things all articles must have to make it successful and helpful in making your site a profit earning and traffic overflowing site.

- Keywords and Keyword Phrases.

An article must always be centered on the keywords and keyword phrases. As each website visitor goes to a site, there are those who are just merely browsing but actually looking for a specific something. When this happens, a searcher usually goes to a search engine and types in the keywords they are looking for (e.g. Toyota Camry, Meningitis, Tax Lawyer and Etcetera). It could be anything they want.

The Important thing is that you have an article that has the keywords that are related to your site. For example, if you maintain an auto parts site, you must be able t have articles about cars and their parts. There are many tools in the internet that provides service in helping a webmaster out in determining what keywords and keyword phrases are mostly sought out. You can use this tool to determine what keywords to use and write about.

- Keyword Density

Know that you have your keywords and keyword phrases, you must use them fully. An article must have good keyword density for a search engine to "feel" its presence. Articles should at least have ten to fifteen percent of keyword density in their content for search engines to rank a site high in their search results. Getting a high rank is what articles do best for a site.

Keyword density is the number of times a keyword or keyword phrase is used on an article. The number varies depending on the number of words used in an article. An effective article must have a keyword density that is not too high or too low. With a very high density, the essence of the article is lost and may turn off a reader as well as the search engines. It comes off as overeager. A low number may be ignored by the search engines.

- Good Article Content

Like what is stated above, you cannot just riddle an article with keywords. They must also be regarded as good reading materials. Articles must be able to entertain people as well as provide good information and help for their needs. Articles should be written well with correct spelling and good grammar. If you want people to trust you, make your work good and well thought out.

People respond well to figures, facts and statistics. Try to get great information and as many facts as you can. A good and well written article will boost your reputation as an expert in your chosen field or topic. As more people believe in you. They will be able to trust you and your products.

- Linking Articles

And another important thing to remember. If you are going to submit articles to ezines and/or contribute your articles to newsletters and other sites, DON'T ever forget to include a link to your site. A little resource box with a brief description of your site and you should always be placed right after your articles that you have submitted. If people like your articles, they will most likely click on the link directing them to your site.

5 Easy Ways To Get Your Creative Juices Going

Writing an article doesn't just mean putting down thoughts into words then typing and writing it. You have to capture the interest of your readers and get them to keep on reading. To send your message across you have to get the attention of the reader and have a firm grasp of their interest and pique their curiosity.

The main ingredient in baking up an article is a large dose of creativity. While creativity may come natural to many people, some just gets into a block or something to that effect that can drive someone crazy. Many writers have literally torn their hair out when they get writers block and just can't seem to get their creative juices flowing.

Putting words into images in the readers mind is an art. A clear and crisp depiction requires a certain flair that only creativity can provide. Similes and metaphors help a lot, but the way an article gets entwined word for word, sentence by sentence then paragraph by paragraph into a whole article develops the essence of the article.

So just what do you have to do when nothing comes to mind? There is no surefire ways to get the perfect ideas but there are easy ways to get your creative juices flowing. No one can guarantee you of having the perfect mindset but many methods may aid you in achieving that state of mind. Here are five easy ways for that.

1) Keep a diary or a journal with you always. Ideas can be triggered by anything you may hear, see, or smell. Your senses are your radar in finding great ideas. Write all of them into a journal and keep it with you for future reference. You may also write down anything that you have read or heard, someone's ideas could be used to develop your own ideas and this is not stealing. Remember that ideas and creativity can come from anywhere; it's the development of the idea that makes it unique.

2) Relax and take time to sort things out. A jumbled mind cannot create any space for new ideas. Everyone must have a clear mind if one wishes to have their creativity in full speed. Get rid of all obstacles that can be a hindrance to your creativity. If you are bothered by something, you cannot force your mind to stay focused.

Try to relax every time that you can and think about your experiences and interactions with others. Your experiences are what shape your mindset and your opinions which could be reflected on your writings. Try to discover yourself, find out what triggers your emotions. Discover what inspires you and what ticks you off. You can use these emotions to help you in expressing yourself and your ideas, with this you can grow creatively.

3) Create a working place that can inspire your creativeness. Your working place can be quite a hindrance if it doesn't make you feel happy or relaxed. Creativity comes from being in a good state of mind and a messed up workplace that causes distraction won't be conducive in firing up your creative flow.

Surround your working place with objects that makes you happy and relaxed. You may put up pictures, or scents, objects that inspire, or anything that can get your creativeness cranking. A clean and well organized workplace also rids of distractions and unwanted hindrances. With a good working place, you can work in peace and never notice the time pass by.

4) Set the mood. Setting the mood requires you to just go with the moment or to induce your self to feeling what makes your mind works best. Finding out what makes you tick could help you find ways to get your creative juices flowing. Set the pace and tempo for your mood and everything else will follow.

There are many ways to set the mood. Some writers have been known to use alcohol, a little sip of wine to stir up the imagination. Some would like some mood music while others let the lighting of the environment create the mood.

5) Go on a getaway and just do something unlike crazy. Letting yourself go and have fun produces adrenaline that can make your imagination go wild. Take an adventure or a solemn hike. Whatever it is that is unusual from your daily routine can take the rut out of your schedule. In no time at all, your creativeness will make use of that experience and get your imagination to go on overdrive.

6 Red Hot Tips To Get Your Articles Read

There are many people who dread having to write papers or articles. Many just feel like it seems to be too much work and it all just goes to waste when no one reads the. To some people, reading articles seems like work to, especially if the article is boring and very bland. Well, articles are supposed to be read, that's their purpose to impart your message and information. If it is not read then it is a waste of time and effort.

But all the same, articles have to be written to be read. It's just a matter of making them good. Making a good article doesn't have to be strenuous and straining. There are just some points needed to be reminded of, and some guides to follow. Once you get the hang of it, writing articles could be fun, as well as profitable for you and your site.

Of course, writing articles must be about something you know about, that's why if you own a site, you probably is knowledgeable about that certain topic and theme. When you write about it, you won't have a hard time because you already know what it is and what it's about. It's just a matter of making your articles creative and interesting.

To make sure that your articles get read and enjoyed, here are six red hot tips to get your articles read. These tips will make your articles readable and interesting.

1) Use short paragraphs. When the paragraph are very long, the words get jumbled in the mind of the reader just looking at it It can get quite confusing and too much of a hard work to read. The reader will just quickly disregard the paragraph and move on to much easier reading articles that are good to look at as well as read. Paragraphs can be a single sentence, sometimes even a single word!

2) Make use of numbers or bullets. As each point is stressed out, numbers and bullets can quickly make the point easy to remember and digest. As each point, tip, guide or method is started with a bullet or point, readers will know that this is where the tips start and getting stressed. Format you bullets and numbers with indentations so that your4 article won't look like a single block of square paragraphs. Add a little bit of flair and pizzazz to your articles shape.

3) Use Sub-headings to sub-divide your paragraphs in the page. Doing this will break each point into sections but still would be incorporated into one whole article. It would also be easy for the reader to move on from one point to another; the transition would be smooth and easy. You will never lose your readers attention as well as the point and direction to where the article is pointing.

4) Provide a good attention-grabbing title or header. If your title can entice a person's curiosity you're already halfway in getting a person to read your article. Use statements and questions that utilize keywords that people are looking for. Provide titles or headers that describe your articles content but should also be short and concise.

Use titles like, "Tips on making her want you more", or "How to make her swoon and blush" .You could also use titles that can command people, for example, "Make her yours in six easy Ways". These types of titles reach out to a persons' emotions and makes them interested.

5) Keep them interested from the start to the finish. From your opening paragraph, use real life situations that can be adopted by the reader. Use good descriptions and metaphors to drive in your point, just don't over do it. Driving your examples with graphic metaphors and similes would make it easy for them to imagine what you are talking about. Making the experience pleasurable and enjoyable for them.

6) Utilize figures when necessary and not just ordinary and insipid statements. Using specific facts and figures can heighten your article because it makes it authoritative. But do not make it too formal, it should be light and easy in them and flow. Like a friendly teac her having a little chat with an eager student.

Articles Are The Quickest Way To Your Customers Wallet

One way of promoting your website and product can be achieved for free. As an additional bonus, this "free" method can boost your sites and sales, doubling and even tripling your income.

Articles. One of the easiest ways to promote your website in order to generate traffic and increase your earnings.

How does this work?

Write articles relating to your website and submit them to "free content" submission sites. Easy to do, takes little time and can increase your website traffic, sales and of course, your income.

How can article writing boost traffic and income?

The article on the free content site contains a link to your own website. Readers, after reading your articles, may choose to click on the link and pay you an unexpected visit. Having them on the free content sites is also making these articles available to other webmasters who may wish to publish that article on their site.

If they do, your article will include a link back to your site. And anyone who reads the article on that site can still click on the link to visit your site.

As the list of your published articles grow larger, and more and more of them are appearing on different websites, the total number of links to your site increases also. Major search engines are placing a lot of significance on incoming links to websites so they can determine the importance of a certain site.

The more incoming links the website has, the more importance search engines attaches to it. This will then increase your website's placement in the search results.

If you site is into promoting a product or service, the links that your articles have achieved will mean more potential customers for you. Even if visitors only browse through, you never know if they might be in need of what you are offering in the future.

There are also those who already have specific things they need on their mind but cannot decide yet between the many choices online. Chances are, they may stumble upon one of your articles, gets interested by the contents you wrote, go to your site and became enticed by your promotions. See how easy that is?

Search engines do not just index the websites, they also index published articles. They also index any article that is written about your own website's topic. So once someone searches for that same topic, the list of results will have your site or may even show the articles that you have written.

And to think, no effort on your part was used to bring them to your site. Just your published articles and the search engines.

It is no wonder why many webmasters are suddenly reviving their old writing styles and taking time to write more articles about their site than doing other means of promotion.

Getting their site known is easier if they have articles increasing their links and traffic and making it accessible for visitors searching the internet. Since many people are now taking their buying needs online, having your site on the search engines through your articles is one way of letting them know about you and your business.

The good thing with articles is that you can write about things that people would want to know about. This can be achieved in the lightest mood but professional manner, with a little not-so-obvious sales pitch added.

If you think about it, only a few minutes of your time is spent on writing one article and submitting to free content site. In the shortest span of time also, those are distributed to more sites than you can think of. Even before you know what is happening, you are getting more visitors than you previously had.

If you think you are wasting your time writing these articles, fast forward to the time when you will see them printed and wide-spread on the internet. Not to mention the sudden attention and interest that people are giving your website and your products or services.

Try writing some articles and you will be assured of the sudden surge in site traffic, link popularity and interest. Before you know it, you will be doubling and even tripling your earnings.

Nothing like getting benefits for something you got for free.

How to Create an Outline For All of Your Article

We've done it through junior high, it expanded longer through high school, then on college it became chapters. No matter how many times a person have done it, writing articles has proven to be a task many has continuously avoided. Now at a time when writing articles could help your job or work, facing the job at hand can be still faced with unfriendly behavior.

While there are a great number of people who do not have the same attitude in article writing as others, there are still those who would rather walk in piping hot coals than do some article writing. What set other people apart from other towards article writing is that they are prepared and has some methods and procedures in writing articles.

One of the methods you can use to prepare yourself when tasked to write in article is creating an outline first. Creating an outline for all your articles makes you prepared. You have an idea of what to do first and make a plan for your succeeding steps. Being prepared makes the job easier and faster. Being organized will allow for disorientation to be shunned away.

An outline can act as the design or blueprint for your article. This will guide you in creating the introduction, body and conclusion of your article. Here in this point, you can write down some of the ideas and sentences that you feel will look good in your article. This could be some of the focal point that could help make your article creative, interesting and appealing to a reader.

A carefully planned and fully prepared project would guarantee and ensure a problem and worry free procedure that can virtually go without any hassles. Creating an outline for all your articles will get you ready and breeze through writing an article in no time at all. Here I will provide you with some tips and guidelines in how to create an outline for all of your articles.

Do a couple of brainstorming and jot down your brilliant ideas first. Think of some ways to attract the interest of your reader. Designate a time frame where you can write down all the ideas that you can use for your articles. By this time you should have done all your research and information searching. Review and reread your ideas and notes, gain mastery and sufficient familiarity with your topic so that writing them down later own would be easy for you.

The next step is to discover your sub topic and sub titles. As you would provide a first sentence for your article, one that would immediately grab the attention of your reader, you would need some as well for your sub topics. To be concise, you would need to get all the facts that will support and go against your point.

These are the frames or skeleton of your article, now its time to add the flesh and the meat of your article. You will need to connect all your paragraphs and sub topics. This will form the body of your Article. While the introduction will usher in the ideas of your paragraph, you will need a conclusion. The conclusion will wrap up your points and drive in what you are saying in your article.

The outline for your article would also require you to write a draft first. This may take more than one attempt but remember that it is called a draft for a reason. Your outline shall be perfected as each draft is written and this draft is meant for your eyes only so there's no reason to feel ashamed. As you go on, you will clearly see the bigger picture and write an article that will perfectly suit what is demanded of it.

Reread and reread what you have written down. Always refer to your outline so that you wont drift away from what you had first written down. Its not hard to be caught in the moment and get lost in your writing frenzy. Your outline will help you keep in track. All those hours spent in outlining your article will not go to waste. This will serve as your guide in writing articles. Trust and rely on your outline because this will prove to be a very helpful tool in writing all of your articles.

I Hate Writing Articles - Isn't There An Easier Way?!

Owning, running and maintaining an internet based business or a site needs articles. Plain and simple, every who has a site knows this. Even those who don't have sites but are frequent internet users knows this as well. Articles quench the thirst for information and knowledge of the people. Plus, the articles provides many other benefits for the site.

The benefits that articles provide are putting a site high in the ranking in search results of keywords and keyword phrases that pertains or are relevant to his or her site. They also provide attraction to website visitors when they are appreciated and is linked to your site from another site or newsletter. Articles provide for the increase of the confidence and trust levels of customers to your site and company.

Many articles are also beneficial to both company and its traffic. When the readers like the articles, they would tell more of their friends, family and peers and recommend your site to them, providing for a larger volume of traffic. You get bigger sales if your traffic trusts and believes in you. Your product or services would be much easier to sell when they know you know what you are doing and talking about.

So ok, we have established that articles are very important to a site and to business. Articles are crucial and to keep ahead in the game, a site must have an article, it is imperative. There is one dilemma though, not many people like writing articles.

Many website owners would rather spend their time on something else, and unless you're a big time company, you don't have the necessary resources to use on a pool of article writers. Plagiarism or copying of other articles is frowned upon and could easily get you into trouble, worst case scenario; a hefty fine and jail time.

So what are the other options?

Well, for starters if you hate writing articles and you can't afford to hire people to write for you then don't. Get free articles. The first place to look at for free articles is the public domain. Here you won't have problems with copyright infringement and the following penalties and fines if you get caught for plagiarism.

Public domain articles are articles freely given to the public for public use. You can do whatever you want with it. You can place it on your site, name it as yours, put it in a newsletter its you decision. Always remember though that you will have to choose articles that is very relevant to your site.

The downside to public domain articles is that since it is free for everybody, many of your competitors may have access to them as well. Since every site needs to be original and unique even though you have the same niche, this could be a predicament. You may also have to edit them a bit to place more keywords and keyword phrases to make them better.

Another way to get free articles is to allow other sites which has the same subject or topic as yours to submit articles to your site. This would be only to augment your existing content or else all your articles would be leading to other sites since these articles would have resource boxes with them that could link or direct the readers to their site. That's why it is important to have your own articles; you cold use them to link your site to other sites as well.

But, to truly feel the impact of what a good article to you, go for original ones. There are many article writers who do part time and freelance article writing jobs that charges only minimal fees. You can get good articles that have all the keywords and keyword phrases you need and people are looking for.

The investment you made for these articles would be worthwhile because you could use them for all the benefits you could offer. You hold copyrights to them and you will be able to use them anyway you want. As your articles help you in building your business and your site, you will have more articles to write and maybe then you wont be having second thoughts about articles.

The easiest Way to Create Articles – Public Domain!

There are many webmasters that find writing articles for their site to be a very tedious task. Many people who need to write articles also procrastinate as much as they can to delay the amount of writing they need to do. Many people dread writing articles because they find researching for the topic and writing down original materials will be too taxing on them.

You need to have your creative juices flowing and simply downloading an article would be plagiarism or tantamount to stealing, not exactly. Have you ever heard about public domain? These are articles written down by many authors that have declared their works to be public domain, which means anybody can use it for whatever purpose they want.

While most authors would prefer to copyright their work for their rights, there are also a number who doesn't mind sharing their work. Public domain articles are not owned by anybody and can be used and abused by anyone. The writers have waived their rights to their works and it is out there for the public to make use of.

You can use public domain articles in helping you write your articles. With the public domain articles you can simply edit them to your own style and rewrite them as you please to make it suitable for your needs. All the ideas are there already and its just a matter of finding the write article with the topic or subject you need.

This is probably the easiest way to write articles. You don't need to scour around the library or the internet for hours for information and start an article from scratch. For webmasters who are looking for articles to fill their site and to generate a high ranking for their website in search engine results, they can just modify the article by infusing keywords and keyword phrases related to their site.

A webmaster or website operator do not risk any chance of getting sued for copyright infringement because they are public domain, once again meaning that anybody can use it. Writing articles by using public domain wont require as much work as writing one from scratch would. You save a lot of time also.

One good factor in using public domain articles for your site or for any project is that you save a lot of money. You dismiss the need to hire experienced and seasoned writers that some website operators use to write their articles. While a single five hundred worded article would only set you down 10 to 15 dollars, this cost will drastically increase when you need hundreds of articles to fill the needs of your site.

For those who needs articles to generate newsletters or an e-zine, public domain articles will be very beneficial. You do not need to count on your contributors or pay writers to write down articles for your newsletter or e-zine. You can fill all the pages without any cost or the worry of being sued and sought after by the writers. You can simply copy the articles and place them on your newsletter and e-zine.

Public domain articles are a virtual untapped resource that many people fail to realize the true value. The power of articles, keywords and keyword phrases have been deemed invaluable these past few years for many internet based businesses and sites that want to rank high in search engine results.

The number of article and content writers have grown significantly due to the rise in the demand for articles. As newer and newer topics and subjects have arisen, there are many demands for new articles to be written. An industry has been formed and this is a worldwide demand.

Public domain articles have given a great alternative for those who are cash strapped as well as do not have the time nor the skills to do their articles for themselves.

Searching for public domain articles is as easy as 1 – 2 – 3. You can search for them in search engines and do searches in many directories for the topic or subject that you need. Read them and simpy copy paste them to a word processing program and simply edit them to suit your needs.

Top Writers Around the World will write for you – outsourcing

The content of your site tells a whole lot about your website. They will basically describe what your site is about and also tell people what your site has to offer. Articles and website content makes a whole lot of difference in your site because they can catch the attention of your website visitors and keep them in there.

With good website content you get the benefit of clearly depicting what it is you want to share with people. Also, good content and articles can lead people to your site. With more traffic, you get to earn more from your site making it profitable. A sites success, be it for profit or not, is the number of the flow of traffic in your site.

So how does good content and great articles get you traffic? Well, many search engines rely on the keyword and keyword phrases of a site to put it in their results list. If your content contains a good number of keywords and keywords phrases, it may be chosen to be a part of the top listed sites in the search result pages.

But before you think of just plastering your site with all the keywords and keyword phrases it could hold, search engines also filter out that abuse. You must have good well written articles that incorporate the keywords and keyword phrases properly in their content and articles.

There are many of those who cannot afford the time to write their own website contents and articles. While writing content and articles specifically designed for the internet may take some getting used to and some researching and learning, there are many writers that can be found all over the world who could do it for you.

Many of us do not have the time to learn web content writing and article writing designed for the internet. There are writers who have great experience in doing this and charge only a minimal fee for such work. Writers like this can be regarded as experts in this style of writing and can greatly help your website to get that coveted spot in the search engine rankings.

Other than getting your site in the web results page of search engines, they can also provide your site with meaningful articles and content that can impress your website visitors and entice others to view your site. Every website could use the extra traffic website visitors could invite.

Then there are those who need papers to be done either for their school or office work. Top writers around the world are very knowledgeable and do extreme researching to get a job done right. They are also very adept in many writing styles that are needed to best suit the client's need.

Many writers around the world charge a minimal fee depending on the type of writing job needed and the number of words needed in the content. Usually, a two hundred fifty worded article would cost from 4 to 8 dollars depending on the writers experience and ability. This is a small price to pay for having a content rich site or for a well researched and written paper.

There are also many sites that can offer you these services with their team of well trained and experienced writers. They offer many writing services to cover any writing needs. A writer can be based anywhere in the world and are guaranteed to offer good contents and articles. Each one are doubly checked, edited and proofread so that you would get your money's worth.

Finding a good writer or a site that offers these kinds of services is simply done by searching for them in search engines. Type down your keyword or keyword phrase (e.g. Content Writers, Article Writers) and you will see a long list of sites that offer these services.

The top sites would probably be the best since they have done a good job of keeping their content at a high quality to get them high rankings. But you may also want to shop around and read some of their sample work to get an idea of how much it will cost you.

Writing the Resource Box so it Makes People click

The internet is the information highway, this phrase has been used so may time it should be nominated for the Internet Cliché Award. People that go to the internet are subdivided into groups, but generally, they are out to search information. Whether for gaming, business, fun or anything else the internet has provided us with information that has proved to be very beneficial.

Through the recent years many people have learned the secrets of Search Engine Optimization. More and more sites have seen the effects articles have done for the traffic of their sites. Some have even created sites devoted entirely to providing articles that could be read by their website visitors and have links that could lead to many sites that are related to the topics and subjects of the articles.

For example, the sites may feature many articles about a whole lot of topics. As a website visitor reads the articles they have searched for, they can find at the end of the article a resource box that can be clicked on to link them to the site that has submitted the article. Of course the article would be in relation to the site. Lets say if the article is about rotating the tires, the resource box may lead to a link to a site that sells tires or car parts.

A resource box is what you usually find at the end of an article. They will contain the name of the author, a brief description of the author, a brief description of the sponsoring site and a link. If a reader likes what they read, they would have the tendency to find out where the article came from to read more. The resource bow will be their link to the source of the article and this will entice them to go to the site and do some more reading or research for the subject or topic they are interested in.

But like the article itself, the resource box must also be eye-catching to demand the attention and interest of the reader. While the resource bow encompasses only a small space, providing the right keywords and content for your resource box will provide more prodding for the reader to go to your site.

Now we know what resource boxes are, what are the benefits of having a good resource box? Mainly its driving traffic to your site. Many sites would allow articles to be placed in their sites because they can make use of the articles to fill their pages. They also get affiliation with other sites that can be beneficial for them as well. For the sponsoring site, when you get people to click on your resource box, you generate traffic that can be counted upon as potential customers.

So what would be a good content for your resource box? Basically it is keywords, learning about the proper keywords that people are mainly searching for. There are many tools you can find in the internet that can help you in determining what keywords to use.

Resource boxes can also make use of all the creativity it can get. You only get a small space for your resource box so you better make the most of it. Try to catch the attention of your reader with resource box content that can make them give a second look. Unlike TV ads, you don't have visual aids to drive your point in. But you do have the power of imagination of a reader. With the right content, you can make them think and intrigued.

Another tip is to use keywords that should be related to your site. Do not mislead your potential website visitors. Build your credibility so that more people would get enticed to visit your site and browse what you have to offer. Make the people click your resource box by providing resource box content that makes a lasting impression. You only get one chance to wow them and hundreds of chances to repulse them.

Never underestimate the power of the resource box. It may be small in size but they will provide a significant aid in driving traffic to your site. A boring resource box will never get a job done. Be fun and creative but at the same time show that you have a great deal to offer, too much to ask for something that couldn't fit a paragraph? Yes and no, there are many tips and guides that can help you in doing this, the first step is realizing how important a resource box could be in making people click your link and be directed to your site.

Opt-In-List

3 Quick And Easy Ways To Build A Profitable Opt In List

You finally realize that you need a good opt-in list. After reading countless articles and sought expert advices and have read many success stories of people creating a small fortune with opt-in lists you finally decide to have one of your own. Then it happens, you think you have known everything there is to know about opt-in lists and have followed their advices to the T and you still weren't able to make a profit.

In fact, you may be losing money. You maybe hiring writers to help you out, or there are some expenses incurred, even if you have a big list, but only a very small percentage actually buys from you, your still losing profit. You'll realize that after a few months when you see your statistics and sales figures.

So what could have gone wrong? Why have others succeeded where you have failed? The most common mistake is that you dived straight right in. You chose a topic where you think could be quite popular and would earn you money. This just not the case. Just because you wrote people from the list doesn't mean they are going to buy instantly.

Here I will offer more advice, for those who have started an opt-in list and have failed, you can rejuvenate your failed venture. For those who are starting, here are three quick and easy ways to build a profitable opt-in list.

1) Get your customers to trust you and your products first. Just launching your opt-in list would not make you an expert and a believable seller. Put many articles first before you start an opt-in list. Write about the topic you know and have started and used for your site. Try to put forums first to gain knowledge about your customers about their wants and needs and target those wants and needs.

Join forums from other sites as well. Provide expert advices and recommendations. When you feel that people trust you already, you will be able to start your own opt-in list. You can build a base as well with other forum users. You can ask them to join your list. Friends are always good customers. Put up a link to your site so that they may be able to see what you're business is all about.

The certain truth is, the money will only come in when the consumers and subscribers believe and trust in you. They want a product or service that could be a good exchange for their money. People are not going to buy something out of your recommendation if they don't know you.

2) Find a product or service that people want and need. Although it may not be your forte, if you provide a service and product that you have researched and learned about well, you can carry it on forward. Invest your time, effort and money that you could sell as well as the buyers or subscribers of your opt-in list can use.

While it is true that it is best to sell something that you have interest in, there are not many people who have the same interest as you if you decide to sell something that is not entirely popular or profitable. Do your research well and you would see the profits come in. Also provide your subscribers with promotional material that they could actually use and spread around.

3) Make friends with other opt-in list users. This is basically beneficial especially if it is someone who has already launched a successful opt-in list. These are people that have the experience in this venture and experience is still the best teacher. While there are many articles available for you in the internet to use, there is nothing like getting a first hand account from someone you trust.

Experienced opt-in list users will be able to tell you what to do and what not to do because they have gone through it. While different situations occur for different people, the general concept can still be very helpful. There are many things to avoid and these people will be able to tell you which ones.

Building a profitable opt-in list don't just happen overnight. There are many preparations and effort to do. Opt-in lists are built from scratch, as your list grows, you should also maintain the quality of your list. Keep it organized and manageable. Get or hire help if need be, just make sure that your subscribers are happy and satisfied and they will be willing to buy from you.

4 Crucial Things You Need To Do To Build your List

Online marketing may have developed a sudden surge these past few years, but many in the know how have felt its rise even from way then. As more internet based businesses are put up, the need to develop new marketing skills and knowledge based on this new medium have arisen. More and more marketing strategies are being discovered and developed to cope with the changing face of business the business world.

The demand for online marketing tips and strategies have drastically grown and a new form of business has been born, internet marketing strategies. While there are companies that are all too eager to help your site and business build a clientele for a fee, there also many ways that can spread the word about your sites subsistence in a more cost free way. One of this is Opt-in email marketing, also known as permission marketing.

Opt-in marketing requires the permission of a willing customer to subscribe to your marketing materials, materials that take form in newsletters, catalogs and promotional mailings via e-mail. The more opt-in marketing mail is sent, the more chances there is to bag sales and more sales. To do this, you must build a list of all those who wants to subscribe to your opt-in marketing list.

From your list, you will get your targeted customer, this is a good list since they already have shown interest in what you have to show and sell since they have willingly signed in for your list. These are the people who have liked what they have seen in your site and have decided they want to see more and maybe even purchase what ever product or service your company and site has to offer.

Many people would think that building their lists would take hard work and a lot of time to build and collect names and addresses. This is not so, it takes a bit of patience and some strategies but in doing this list, you open your site and your business to a whole new world of target market. Take the effort to take your business to a new level, if traffic increase and good profits are what you want, an opt-in list will do wonders for your business venture.

There are many sources and articles in the internet available for everyone to read and follow in building a list. Sometimes they may be confusing because there are so many and there different ways. Different groups of people would have different approaches in building an opt-in list, but no matter how diverse many methods are, there are always some crucial things to do to build your list. Here are four of them.

1) Put up a good web form in your site that immediately follows the end of your content. While some may say this is too soon to subscribe for a website visitors application, try to remember that your homepage should provide a quick good impression. If somehow a website visitor finds something that he or she doesn't like and turns them off, they may just forget about signing up.

A good web form for subscribing to an opt-in list is not hard to do. Just write a simple short statement about how they would like to see more and get updated about the site. Then there should be an area where they could put in their names and e-mail address. This web form will automatically save and send you the data's inputted. As more people sign in, your list will be growing.

2) As mentioned in the first tip, make your homepage very, very impressive. You need to have well written articles and descriptions of your site. Depending on what your site is all about, you need to capture your website visitor's fancy. Make your site useful and very easy to use. Do not expect everyone to be tech savvy. Invest in having good programming in your site, make your graphics beautiful but don't over do it.

Don't waste your time making the homepage too overly large megabyte wise. Not all people have dedicated T1 connections, the faster your site gets loaded, the better. Go for a look that borders between simplicity and sophisticated knowledge.

3) Provide good service and products. A return customer is more likely to bring in more business. Even then and now, a satisfied customer will recommend a business always. Word of mouth and recommendations alone can rake in more business than an expensive ad. As your clientele roster grows so shall your list. With more members on the list, the more people will get to know about what you have new to offer.

4) Keep a clean and private list. Never lose the trust your customers have entrusted you. If you provide e-mails to others and they get spammed, many will probably unsubscribe to you. Remember, a good reputation will drive in more traffic and subscribers as well as strengthen the loyalty of your customers.

4 Ways To Get Your Opt In Subscribers To Trust You Quickly

While the rest of the world have developed many barriers and protections to keep their e-mail accounts spam-free, there are also those that subscribe to mails that promotes their products, services and their site. This is mainly because these subscribes wants to know more about what these sites are offering and can be beneficial for them. They expect to get be kept posted on what they are interested in and what are new in the market or field they have chosen.

Businesses would be so lucky to have these kinds of customers; the basic element needed to get these types of people is trust. When your customers trust you they will reward you with their loyalty. Many internet users have gone to great lengths in protecting their email accounts from spam mail. Some free-mail internet providers and internet service providers offer spam protection while there are also some internet based companies that screen your mails for you.

With an opt-in mail list, the mails you send containing your promotional materials such as newsletters, catalogs and marketing media will go through. Your intended recipient will be able to read and view what you have sent making it a successful transfer of information. To be able to be allowed to do so, you will need permission from your recipient, to get this permission; you need to be able to get their trust. With the great lack of disregard for privacy in the internet, getting the trust of an internet user you don't personally know is a big achievement.

To build a good opt-in list you need people to trust you, for a faster and quicker build up, you need to get your opt-in subscribers to trust you quickly. The faster you build your opt-in list the faster word about your site and company gets to be spread. The bigger the scope of your opt-in list the more traffic you get spelling more profits. Its easy math if you thin about it. Getting the numbers is not that simple though, or maybe it is?

- Getting the trust of your clientele shouldn't be so hard especially if you do have a legitimate business. Getting your customers trust should be based upon your expertise. People rely on other people who know what they are talking about. Garner all the knowledge and information about your business. Ell, frankly if you decide to go into a business most probably you have an interest in it. Like how many basketball payers become coaches, you don't really venture into something you don't have any interest in.

- Show your clients that you know what you are talking about. Provide them with helpful hints and guidelines that pertain to what you are selling. Talk about how to install a roof if your into hardware products or provide articles on insurance settlements if you're a settlement lawyer. You don't have to be a big corporation to make use of an opt-in list. If your customers see you as someone who knows what he is doing and saying, they will trust you quickly.

- Be true to your customers, if you want to hype up your products and services, provide guarantees. The more satisfied customers you get, the bigger probability there is that they will recommend you. Generally, people will trust someone they know, when that someone recommends you then you're a shoo-in. They will go to your site and check it for themselves and be given a chance to experience what the other shave experienced from you, so make sure to be consistent in the service you provide.

- Another tip in getting a customer to trust you quickly is to provide them an escape hatch. Show them that you are not there to trap them. Keep a clean list that would enable them to unsubscribe anytime they want. Elaborate your web form by providing information on how to unsubscribe from the list. Guarantee them that they can let go of the service when ever they want to. Many are wary that they may be stuck for life and would have to abandon their email accounts when they get pestered with spam.

Remember that when you get the trust of your clients don't lose that trust. Because if you do anything with their email addresses like sell them or give them out, you will lose many members of your list as ell as potential members. The true quickest way to gain the trust of your subscribers is when you are recommended by someone they trust.

5 Things To Consider When Publishing A Newsletter

Providing a newsletter for your opt-in list subscribers provides many benefits in terms of driving traffic into your site as well as boosting the sales and profits of your site and company. This is a marketing ploy that will not hugely dent your marketing budget and will not also require many man-hours in developing this project.

With a newsletter, you can inform the public about your company and products as well as services. You can keep them posted and updated about what's going-on with your company as well as many of your promotions and offerings. With these, you keep on reminding your subscribers that you are still here and is willing to offer them good deals and services.

Newsletters also allow you to impress your subscribers. It can show your expertise and knowledge about the topic at hand and the many benefits you can offer them. When you impress people, they will become potential customers and another great thing is that they can recommend you to their friends, colleagues and family. All of them could very well be customers in the future.

If you do not have a newsletter or publishing one for your site, then you may have to consider about researching and be well informed on how to publish one. It is not as easy as it seems but if and when you get the right idea and process, it will be smooth sailing from there on. Try to take the time to learn what you need to learn and get that newsletter ready and good to attract subscribers to your newsletter as well as traffic to your site.

In the next few paragraphs, I will provide you with some things to reflect on when you decide to start your own newsletter for your site. Here are five things to consider when publishing a newsletter.

1) Make sure that the content of your newsletter pertains to and closely associated with your business or the theme of your site. Do not dwell too far on what could be regarded as your field of expertise. You have started a site and your theme for your site will always be something you are knowledgeable about. For example; if you have a site that sells auto car parts, your newsletter must contain articles or content like photos that pertain to cars, auto parts and such. You may also include content about your company and your staff.

Remember that visitors of a certain site are there because they are interested in what the site has to offer. If they sign up for an opt-in list or for a newsletter this means that they want to be updated for that certain theme or subject. Be sure that when you publish your newsletter you are providing for the need of the subscriber as well as their interests.

2) Ensure that you have well written, information riddled and content rich articles. You articles will be the body of your newsletter and that they should be able to excite your readers as well as provide information. Articles should be well written and checked for errors such as spelling and grammatical errors for it to look professional and believable. The trust of your client to you and newsletter is at stake here.

3) Fact-check your articles. Make sure that you provide true facts and figures so that your reputation as an expert and knowledgeable in that field is not questioned. If you lose the trust of your subscribers these may persuade them to unsubscribe to your newsletter. You will lose many potential sales this way.

4) Provide fresh and new articles that can provide new information to your subscribers. If you publish stale and old news in your newsletter, there is a tendency that people or your subscribers already have read and known about them. This will lose their interest in your newsletter and they wont get to read what is most important, your ads. They may not open or read any of your succeeding newsletters losing your intention in writing and publishing newsletters, to get them to visit your site and make a purchase.

5) Never use copyrighted materials such as photos and articles. This is outright plagiarism, you may get into a lot of trouble for this. You can lose your business and get sued over copyright infringement. If you do not have the time to write your own articles, there are many willing and able professional article writers that can do it for you for a reasonable fee. All your investment in writing and publishing articles will be well worth it when you see your list build up and your traffic increasing.

7 Ways To Make Money Using Nothing More Than Your List

An opt-in list can be quite crucial to any site or internet based company. Even for a small venture such as a niche profit site an opt-in list can make a world of difference and also add some extra income for your pocket. Rarely would you see an e-commerce site, big or small, that is without an opt-in list.

An opt-in list allows for a company to market their wares and site via an e-mail. With an opt-in list, a site and a subscriber consents to sending and receiving a newsletter from your company. Through this, you can keep your subscribers abreast of what is currently available in your site as well as whatever is coming out.

And because there is mutual consent between the two parties, any mail sent to the list is not considered as spam mail. There is a great number of successfully read promotional materials such as catalogs, newsletters and such that are sent because the subscribers themselves have signed up for them, meaning, they do want to be sent those items.

Building a list is crucial, only a small percentage actually subscribes for an opt-in list. Many people find promotional mails annoying but of you provide a good newsletter or promotional material, you will see your list build up and grow. You can also achieve this by having good content on your site. If people like what they see and read on your site, then they surely would want more. Newsletters would be a way to attract them back to your site. A little teaser or appetizer if you will.

But other than marketing your wares and your services, an opt-in list can also be used to earn extra profit. Not all lists can be used though. It would be good to first build a successful list with a huge number of subscribers. The more subscribers you have, the more money you can get. Here are seven ways to make money using nothing more than your list.

1) Place advertisements. There are many corporations who will be willing to pay to put their banners and ads on a list with many subscribers. Selling or renting out lists is not a good idea so rather than doing that, many companies would just rather place ads with lists that have a huge subscriber base. Your newsletter could be placed with many ads and each one spells money.

2) Have affiliations with other companies that have at least a semblance or relation to what your site is about. Here other companies will provide links and brief descriptions of what they offer, products and services. With every click made on the link that directs or leads a subscriber from your list to their site, the company will pay you. This P4P or pay for performance.

3) Make deals with other companies by asking for a small percentage of sales done through your list. With every sale done by customers that have come from your list and have gone there because of your newsletter, the other company will pay you a small percentage of your sales. The more people who buys from them, the more earnings you get.

4) You may also get products from other sites on a consignment basis and sell them to your list via your newsletter. Place descriptions, articles and photos of the product in your newsletter. There will be those who will buy from you and when that happens, you can order the product from the other site and sell it to your buyer.

5) Sell e-books or a compilation of your articles on your list. Manuals and how-to articles are in great demand. Many people will be willing to shell out money to gain knowledge about a certain topic and subject. With your existing list trusting your expertise in that area, an e-book could be offered and sold or used as an incentive.

6) Create a network out of your list. Get people to invite more people to view your site and subscribe to your list. The larger your list is, the more people will be able to click on your links and affiliate links as well as make your advertisement rates higher.

7) Subscribers are willing to pay for information if they know that it can be trusted and relied upon. Use your list to get more and more people to subscribe to you as well as browse your site. Lastly, you can use your list to earn money by making them your partners. Your list will be the bloodline of your growth and increase.

Can You Really Use Articles To Build Your List?

Getting customers in your site should always be ranked as high as the importance of the quality and the excellence of the product and the services you provide. They should go hand in hand in providing your customers the satisfaction they get in exchange for the money they have paid for them. Customer service should as well be as fantastic so that the customers are provided with the same satisfaction.

One of the ways you can combine marketing and customer service is through opt-in marketing. With an opt-in list you get the opportunity to introduce your site and products on a good time basis. Opt-in marketing strategy is a marketing strategy that is virtually low cost and not time consuming. Here, you get the consent of your website visitors to subscribe to your newsletters and other promotional materials such as catalogs and free promotions.

Opt-in marketing uses your list of subscribers to send e-mail to. These e-mails will contain the materials you will send to your subscribers. It is essential that you present your promotional items in a manner that will catch the interest and the eye of your subscribers to keep them wanting for more. The best way to do this is to provide fun, entertaining and informational articles.

Well written articles full of content and useful information will help in building your list as more subscribers will be enticed your list. When they have read the samples of your contents in your sites, they will be intrigued as to what will come next. Subscribing to your newsletter will offer them a glimpse of what you have to offer next.

Many sites and companies have captured the importance of articles and this also aids in search engine optimization. As more people are heading towards the internet for their information needs, serving the right information to them via articles in your site will increase the flow of your website traffic. With more traffic, the percentage of your sales will grow. More sales turn into more profit.

There have been the rise for the importance of well written, information enriched and keyword packed articles for the content of their site as well as for newsletters. These articles provide the information many are seeking in the internet. If your site has them, more people will be going to your site for information and research.

Well written articles would also boost your sites reputation. If they are filled with many information you will be regarded as well informed and an expert on the subjects that you tackle. Your articles must be well researched so that the people will trust you. When you have gained their trust, they will always come for you for their needs on that subject.

In connection, you must write articles or commission them to tackle subjects that are closely connected with your type of business. If you have a site for a medicine tackling a certain disease, your articles must be about the diseases. Or if you sell materials for home improvements provide articles with those themes. Most articles searched for are tips, guidelines, methods, manuals and such. If you provide these articles to your customers and you have their trust, they will always go to your site for help and advice as well as for your products.

With the loyalty of these customers, they may subscribe to your opt-in list to receive all the information you have. If you provide them with the answers for that need, they will be happy to be receiving your newsletters as well as other promotional materials to keep them well informed. Others may even forward your newsletters to other people when they find a certain article interesting.

You should provide links in your newsletter so that when other people are reading it and wants to read more, they may click on the link and go to your site. With the articles you have in your site that are good, they may decide to sign up as well for your opt-in list. This will build your list and make it bigger.

Make sure to keep your subscribers happy and interested in your newsletters and promotional materials. Keep on posting and writing good articles for your site and newsletter. If you are not interested in writing them or if you just don't have the time, there are many available well experienced and knowledgeable writers available to help you out. This is an investment that will pay for itself in time.

How To Build A List Of Eager Subscribers

Every online business provides great service to generate satisfaction among their customers. As each and every customer receives satisfaction over their products or the services they get, there is a great chance that they will become a return customer and buy again. Better yet, they will recommend you to other people that could generate more business for you and your site.

As more traffic is driven to your site, you can entice many of them to subscribe to your mailing list or opt-in list. This is a list where in website visitors agree to be sent promotional materials such as newsletters, catalogs and such that could keep them updated about your site or the niche of your site. These promotional materials are sent via e-mail to the members of the list in different time intervals.

When using e-mail as the media of your marketing and advertisements, you eliminate the need for high costs. Email is free and if you can manage to make your own promotional advertisements you can also save a bundle there. With an opt-in subscribers list, you are pretty sure that what you are sending out is received, viewed and read by the subscribers and not simply being deleted. They have signed up for service and have consented in receiving it.

This means that there are constant reminders to your subscribers about all your products, new products and services as well as any promotions and special deals you are having. There is also the chance that they can be forwarded to other potential customers as they tell their friends and families about you and your site.

Of course you should be also aware that a subscriber may unsubscribe when they feel that they are not getting what they want or expected. Make sure that they are satisfied with your opt-in marketing strategies and keep them excited in receiving your newsletters and catalogs. Here are some tips that can help you build a list of eager subscribers.

Make your promotional materials interesting and fun. Try to use a little creativity but not too over artsy. Build around what your product or service is about. For example; if you are selling car parts, put some pictures of what is new in the auto parts world, a new wing door possibly that can fit any car and make it look like a Lamborghini.

Try to research what people are looking for, these way, you stay one step ahead of them all the time and you will be their bearer of new tidings. They will be eager to receive what you are sending them because they new you always have fresh and new things to share with them.

Write good articles that can be very informational but light at the same time. If your subscribers enjoy your articles, they will go to your site by clicking the links that you will be putting on your newsletter to read some more. You can provide articles that can connect to many people. Be diverse in your articles. Put something humorous, then put something informational, then put something that has both.

Are you wary about this because you don't like writing? No problem, there are many professional and experienced article writers that can do the job for you for minimal fees. They know what they are doing and can provide the need that you have for your newsletters, the money that you pay for your articles are going to be met by the many sign-ups and the potential profit from the sales that you will get.

Create and send an E-book to your customers about anything that is related to your business or site. Use your knowledge and expertise in the field you have chosen to help other people who are similarly interested. Offer this e-book for free. You can write about anything informational and helpful to your subscribers. For example; you can do manuals and guides in so many things. This e-book could be used as a reference for many people.

Share this e-book with everyone, even other sites; just make sure that they don't change the links in the e-book that will lead people to your site. If you want, you can always get some people to write it for you just like your articles. Your investment once again will be covered by the great marketing this will generate.

Add e-coupons in your newsletters that will help them avail to special discounts. Put a control number in your e-coupon so that they can only be used once. When people get discounts that can be found in your newsletters, they will be eager to receive your newsletter in anticipation of what you are promoting next.

If your subscribers can get benefits from your newsletters, they will be very eager to receive them. Just don't flood your mailing list with mails so that you don't annoy your subscribers.

How To Get Your Subscribers Begging For More

Just as an experiment, a friend of mine subscribe to ten different opt-in e-mail marketing lists to see which ones are effective. Many websites and online businesses have resorted to sending promotional materials to people who have subscribed to them in an effort to boost their sales or traffic. Opt-in email marketing sends newsletters, catalogs updates and many more promotional materials to website visitors who have agreed to be updated whether monthly, weekly or semiannually.

Through e-mail, an internet user that is on the list will receive their updates through email. If a promotional material piques their interest they will go to the site to learn more or to purchase outright. For the website operators or owners, this is a chance to remind their list of their existence and parlor their wares. With the numerous sites in the internet that offers the same products or services in one way or the other, the competition can get pretty tight and it is easy to be forgotten.

Back to my experimenting friend, he tried to find out which opt-in marketing strategies grabbed a person into begging for more. Some would send in very simple fashion, some would very outlandish while there are some that would just lie in between. The differences could easily be noticed and some have gotten the idea of an effective opt-in marketing strategy. He dubbed them effective because he felt like he just couldn't wait to go their site and learn more, the more persuasive ones even got him halfway to reaching for his wallet and to his credit card before he realized this was only for an experiment.

Many companies and site present their promotional materials in a wide variety of concepts. Each has their own distinctive style and designs, but more than the outline and the presentation, the content and the articles are what keeps the attention of your potential customer locked on to your opt-in marketing medium. Creativity is the key here.

From talking to many satisfied opt-in list subscribers and forums, I have learned of what is essential in opt-in marketing and what makes the subscribers begging for more instead of lining up to unsubscribe.

Keep your promotional materials light, creative and original. Many people are stressed out as it is. Getting a stuffy business proposal rather than a light hearted e-mail may just agitate them more. A warm friendly smile or banter is always more welcome than a serious business meeting or proposal. While you do want your customers to take you and your products and services seriously, you also want to show them that you know how to have fun.

Splash some color in your emails as well as provide some photos and articles that can be related to you but show good news or good light hearted images as well. Provide a newsletter or promotional materials that will keep them in a light mood. Make your materials eye catching and grabbing that they wont be able to take their eyes of them. Pique their interests.

Have good content and article, even if it means investing in an experienced and professional copy writer to write them for you. An effective copy writer should be able to build trust between you and your customers. They should be able to establish your credibility in what they write. It must be informative but not too stuffy. Let go of the professional jargons and "talk"to your recipients.

A good article and content should be able to outline the benefits of your product and services and why they need what you are offering. But do not look to be overeager and too persuasive. It should be able to entertain as well as lead them to buying from you.

Your promotional materials should be clear. Don't leave people guessing. You should lead them to you and not vice versa. Explain to them what they need to do in a manner that won't be confusing. Try to anticipate also what your target client needs. Do your research and information gathering, many sites will be able to help you with that.

Provide clear and crisp images of what you are offering. If the people know what you have for them, they are more likely to beg for more. For example, if you are selling a car, provide them photos but only enough to encourage them to go to your site for more.

How To Grab Your Readers Attention With Your Subject

The race for supremacy in the internet based businesses has been really heating up and many sites have been put up to help others to get ahead for a small fee. But there are also ways in which you don't have to pay so much to make yourself a good list of loyal followers. Having a satisfied web traffic and visitors allows you to put up a foundation wherein you can build an opt-in list and make it grow from there.

An opt-in list allows you to provide newsletters to your subscribers with their consent. When people sign up, they know that they will be receiving updates and news from your site and the industry your represent via an e-mail. But that doesn't mean that all of those who subscribe read them at all. Many lists have been built due to an attachment with free software or for a promotional discount and such. Some are not really interested in receiving e-mails from companies and just treat them as waste of cyberspace and delete or trash them without so mush as opening the e-mail and scanning them.

You can change all that. While forwarding an email message is relatively after producing your newsletter. Getting people to open them is not as easy. You don't want to waste all the time and effort used in making the newsletters, you want people to read them and have their interests piqued. Interested enough to go to your website and look around and most especially purchased and acquire your products or services.

One of the numerous ways you can tempt or persuade your subscriber is by providing a well thought out and well written subject. The subject of an email is what is often referred to when a person or a recipient of an email decides whether he or she wants to open or read an e-mail. The subject could easily be regarded as one of the most important aspect of your promotional e-mail.

Your subject must be short and concise. They should provide a summary for the content of the e-mail so that the recipient will have basic knowledge of the content. This is really vital in grabbing the attention of your readers and subscribers. You want your subject to instantly grab the attention of your subscriber and get them to be intrigued to open up your mail. Remember, it is not necessarily true that a subscriber opens up subscribed mails.

A good subject must always be tickling the curiosity of your recipient. It must literally force the recipient to open the mail. A certain emotion must be ignited and get them to open the mail. It is essential to use specific words to get the reaction you need. Keep in mind that the recipient or subscribers spends only a few seconds looking over each subject of the e-mails he receives. You must grab your reader's attention right away.

There are many forms you can use for your subject. You can provide a subject that says your e-mail contains content that teaches them tips and methods on certain topics. An example of this is using keywords and keyword phrases such as, "How to" , "tips", "Guides to", Methods in and others like that.

You can also put your subject in a question form. These may include questions like, "Are you sick and tired of your job?" Or "Is your boss always on your case?" Try to stay on the topic that pertains to your site so that you'll know that your subscribers have signed up because they are interested in that topic. This form of subject is very effective because they reach out to your recipients emotions. When they have read the question on your subject, their mind starts answering the question already.

You can also use a subject that commands your reader. Statements such as "Act now and get this once in a lifetime opportunity", or "Double, triple and even quadruple what you are earning in one year". This type of subject deals with the benefits your company provides with your product and services.

You may also use breaking news as your subject to intrigue your subscriber. For example, if you deal with car engine parts you can write in your subject, "Announcing the new engine that uses no gasoline, It runs on water". This creates curiosity with the reader and will lead them to open the mail and read on.

The 3 Things To Avoid When Emailing Your List

When you decide to have an opt-in list, it is not just a matter of sending your subscribers your promotional newsletters or catalogs. There are many things to consider in avoiding many complications. While there are so many ways you can make people subscribe to your list, there are also some things you must do to avoid subscribers from wanting to get off from your list.

Aside from that, you also want to avoid any problems with the law and your internet service provider or ISP. There are now many laws and rules that are applied to help protect the privacy of the internet users from spamming and unwanted mails. With the popularity of the electronic mail as a medium for marketing because of the low cost, many company's have seized the opportunity and have flooded many people's e-mail accounts with promotional mail.

But, with an opt-in list, you avoid this annoyance because people subscribe to the list; they want to receive the newsletters and promotional materials. They have consented to being on the list by subscribing themselves, just don't forget to put an unsubscribe feature everytime in your opt-in list so that you avoid any confusion. There may be times when an email account was provided when the real owner didn't want to subscribe.

It is essential that you keep your list clean and manageable. Arrange it by using the many tools and technologies available for your opt-in list. Do not worry; your investment in this marketing strategy is well worth it with all the coverage you will get which will likely be converted into sales then to profit.

Keep yourself and your business out of trouble and potential run-ins with the law and the internet service providers. Keep your operation legit and clean. Your reputation as a legitimate businessman and a legitimate site depends on your being a straight and true marketing strategist. As a tip, here are three things to avoid when emailing your list.

1) Take notice of your unsuccessful sends. These are the e-mails that bounce. Bounced emails, also known as undeliverable messages, are those messages that, for whatever reason, were not successfully received by the intended recipient.

There are bounces that happen or occur because the server was busy at that time but can still be delivered in another time. There are also bounces because the inbox of the recipient is full at that time. There are those bounce messages that are simply undeliverable ever. The reason for this is that it may be an invalid email address, a misspelled email address, or an email address that was abandoned and erased already.

Manage your list by putting markings on those that bounce. Erase an email account from your list so that you have an accurate statistics and records as to how many are actually receiving your mail. You may also want to check the spellings of your email addresses in your list. One common mistake is when an N instead of an M is placed in the .com area.

2) Always provide an unsubscribe feature in your site and an unsubscribe link in your mails. When someone in your list files a request to be unsubscribed, always take that request seriously. If you don't take them off your list and keep sending them your e-mails, you are now sending them spam mail.

When you are reported as a spammer, you and your business can get into a lot of trouble. You can be reported to the authorities and maybe blacklisted by many internet service providers. You will lose a lot of subscribers this way and many more in potential subscribers.

3) Do not provide pornographic or shocking and disturbing content in your newsletters. It is hard to decipher the age of the recipient and many complaints may stem from these. Controversial issues also are to be avoided to not be branded by your subscribers. Stick to the nature of your site and business.

Always remember these tips in this article so that you can have a healthy relationship with your subscribers as well as be kept within the boundaries of what is allowed in sending mails to an opt-in list.

25 Various Tips

Affiliate Marketing: Why is it One of the Most Cost-Effective Ways to Advertise your Business

Ever heard of affiliate programs? These are forms of Internet advertising that rewards the affiliates for driving traffic to the advertiser or for other transactions. The advertiser pays the affiliate to place a link on their website, and the affiliate sends traffic to the advertiser in return. Simply put, it's about paying commissions to people who help you make sales. It's that easy. NOT.

Affiliate marketing has its ups and downs. It could be draining if you are not armed with updated information and the technical how-tos. But this article's sole objective is to reach out to you and not to badmouth affiliate marketing.

Here are the following reasons on why web marketers go gaga over affiliate marketing as a form of Internet advertisement.

1. Low cost

Many are scared to go on a home based business because of the capital required. In affiliate marketing, you don't have to spend much to start raking in moolah.

2. Inventories not included

Product management fuss could be very stressing. An inventory is not asked to be maintained. The merchant does the maintenance required.

3. Unlimited income through leverage

When you have a paid job, your monthly income mainly relies on whether you go to work or not. With affiliate marketing, your affiliates could all just lead traffic to your site without having to lift a finger after providing them your ad copy and links. Though not every web marketer earns limitless, it still is a fact that all the necessary matters for the advertiser or Internet marketer are all there to be successful.

4. Go worldwide

With affiliate marketing, you are dealing with a global market place. All you have to do is choose a niche product and prepare all the necessary tools for your affiliates to lead traffic from just about anywhere to your website.

5. Low risk

The very main reason for Internet marketer's enthusiasm with affiliate marketing is its having a low risk factor. Especially for those with low budget set aside for advertising, affiliate marketing is just the way to do it.

6. No closing time

With affiliate marketing, your business works every single second of the day while targeting a worldwide market! What could be better than that?

But all of these will be put to waste if you don't have the right niche product and all the other important tools to make it big in affiliate marketing, i.e., well-SEO-ed website. So better work on this first before ever considering those benefits.

Writing Articles as an Affordable Internet Marketing Method

From Overture, a keyword suggestion tool, you will see the millions of searches done to a certain keyword. When these keywords are typed on search boxes of search engines, indexed websites containing articles with those keywords will be displayed. And this is what leads traffic to websites with keyword-rich articles. Yes, the magic word is articles.

Content is king. You can say that again. That is why writing articles is one of the most utilized Internet marketing media today. Internet surfers just can't get enough of information on various fields. Providing information through these articles is a surefire way to drive hot traffic to your web site.

Why is this so? Here are the benefits that writing articles can give your Internet business.

1. It's absolutely free.

Too good to be true? Not. Okay, you have to pay for your Internet Service Provider. That's it. All you need is your thoughts, your computer, and your hands. If you have those, nothing will stop you from typing words that will make you complete that article for your website. On which aspect of that process did you really shell out any cent? Maybe later when your electric bills come.

2. Your website will be noticed in a short period of time.

Submit that article of yours to article directories that get the most web traffic and in no time your web site will be crawled. That is if you don't forget including your resource box or byline.

3. Obtain back links automatically.

When you submit your articles to directories, surely, other websites will make use of your article too. With the copyright terms of your articles, the URL of your website will still be in tact and will subsequently direct more traffic to your website.

4. Improve your reputation.

As an Internet marketer, if you plainly display your products on your website, you will not gain much conversion rate. Conversion is when your traffic converts to sales. You have to show that you are knowledgeable on your field. And what better way to show that than by writing articles that will allow you some bragging rights, right?

Just make your creative juices flow and jot down or key in those ideas quickly to jumpstart your article writing momentum. With those benefits listed above, a writer's block is the last problem you will ever be able to surmount.

Best Internet Marketing Solutions Without Overspending

The Internet has made this world an open enterprise. It has become important for companies to further expand their market and their consumer targets. Engaging to Internet Marketing maybe a risk for people who wish to be involved with this type of business.

Ensure that most of your target consumers will surely acquire your product. Consider the best products which will definitely capture their interests and needs. This means that you need to identify specifically who these people are, their location and financial level in the society. Have a marketing knowledge and skill to achieve your goal in the field of Internet marketing.

At the present, you can use varied Internet Marketing Solutions that is being offered by companies which can be your tool for support to your consumers. This solution maybe email marketing, search engine optimization or creating web pages or sites. Since you need to maximize your return profit, you need to choose Internet Marketing Solutions that will help you achieve this. These marketing techniques will not cost much since they are very self-explanatory, thus, learned easily.

Email marketing is a common Internet marketing Solution. This is a cost effective way of communicating and interacting to your consumers, driving them to visit your website and check out your products. It may be in a way of marketing articles, leading them to forums or newsletters. A newsletter has an advantage of expanding your consumers as more and more sign up on it until you can have a bulk list of emails.

Another great Internet marketing solution is through websites. This is a good promotion strategy to employ since you can display all the necessary information for your target consumers. The website should capture their interest and be complete since every transaction, from inquiry to payments may take place. All correspondence that will be done online must be well-facilitated by the features of your website.

Another Internet marketing solution is search engine optimization. This is a type of service for your website that you can make use of in order to raise the number of visitors to your site. Once a consumer uses a search engine, your website will rank high in the list of searches which in return will increase your site's traffic.

Considering these Internet Marketing Solution, there are different companies offering software products containing one or all of these solutions. It would be a great opportunity to try one of these which will match your financial capability and expected return profit.

Blogging: Free Internet Marketing Method

It's been years since blogging has been practiced. But it's just recently that it has been considered as one of the addicting fads. Many teenagers have resorted to blogging as an outlet for their emotions, a little online nook where they can blurt out whatever just bugs them or whatever makes them feel elated. Savvy marketers have discovered that blogging is one of the best Internet marketing methods that won't cost you a cent.

What exactly is blogging? Blog is the widely used term that refers to web log. Basically, a blog is an online journal. A blog could be set up to no cost at all, and can be used for just for the fun of it or for business reasons.

Blogging for your Internet business is one surefire way to boost the visibility of your products and services. Here are a few ways to boost your internet advertising with the help of a blog:

1. Make your clients or customers abreast on your website's alterations. Your new products and affiliate websites could also be announced through your blog.

2. Keep track of your business objectives and plans through open writing. Your blog content can be easily stored through archives. What could be better than searchable information that could be easily accessed by anyone browsing the web, right?

3. Air your opinions, advice or reviews on specific services or products that are related to your business. Publishing is a very easy process with blogging.

4. Include links that will fetch back links and subsequently improve your ranking on search engines. This could be better executed through putting well-written articles in your website. Affiliate links could also be included in your blog to earn more extra income.

5. Collect response through the ability of blogs to fetch comments from your blog readers. You can learn and improve your products and services through with the feedback from your readers.

6. Connect easily with other bloggers. When other bloggers notice that you have something good in your blog, they will put you in their favorite lists that will automatically link you to their blogs.

So, how do you set up a blog? Here are some of the options you can make use of to take advantage of this fun way to advertise your Internet business.

Either you load a blogging software or let a blogging hosting service do it for you. Host services such as LiveJournal and Blogger.com are the most popular in this field. Those hosts will provide you with easy instructions on how to put up your blog.

How to Make Use of Cheap Internet Banner Advertising

For years now, internet banner advertising has captured the World Wide Web for it has become a large help in saving an amount of money while reaching beyond territories. Banner advertising played a major part in market trafficking all over the internet and many individuals and companies have bought themselves these cheap internet banner advertising. Some made use of it financially; others have no idea on what to do with it.

With your cheap internet banner advertisement, would you just sit in front of your computer and wait for people to notice you? Would you let your company get trampled by other company's marketing strategies?

Okay, so you admit you bought internet banner advertising, but does that mean you won't do anything about it because it costs cheap?

These following steps will help you get up on your feet and make your cheap internet banner advertising priceless. With these simple instructions, there will always have traffic on your website.

First, to be able to capture the attention of your target audience, your title and topic should be thought of with concern. You have to make the people believe that your cheap internet banner advertising is worthy of their time. The advertisement has to meet the audience's need.

For the people to bring attention to your internet banner advertising, you should be able to raise the curiosity and convince the people. You should be able to deliver your products or services with strong words that may lead the target audience at deciding.

You should be able to constructs words on your advertisements that could lead the target audience that you are directly talking to them to give a sense of familiarity on your services.

As you persuade the people by calling for them and directing them to buy or entail your services, they give importance to your business proposal. Your cheap internet-based banner advertising will become one of the sought for ads there are.

Make sure to present your ads to the global community repeatedly to get them familiar with you and your services.

Always remember that having a website doesn't mean it could sell products by itself. You must be sure to accompany it with marketing strategies. By buying banner advertising, you or your company would save time and money while achieving market sales. These internet banners advertising may come cheap, but it could lead you or your company to riches.

Email Marketing: Affordable Internet Marketing Technique

Email marketing is labeled as a killer method when it comes to effective low-cost Internet marketing endeavors. This is because it is the most widely-used and has the best reputation in bringing targeted traffic to websites. It is used to stay in touch with your customers or prospective customers, send out invitations, or make special offers.

It's as easy as writing an e-mail that may be in a form of a newsletter or a plain announcement, and sending that to as many targeted recipients as possible. However, there's an ideal way of going about it. Email marketing is not just about writing any email that you will be sending to anybody. To clarify that, here are some simple tips in doing email marketing the best way possible.

1. Join the "Can Spam" campaign.

Email marketing is not at any rate tantamount to spamming. You are not supposed to send information that your email list will not have any valuable use for.

2. Make your email list open it.

Your email might get lost together with the hundreds of emails that inbox owners are confronted with everyday. Improve your subject line by using extra white space creatively, adding text symbols, starting each word with a capital letter, asking compelling questions, not making any unbelievable claims, and not using the word FREE.

3. Keep it real.

Not including any too good to be true statements is not only applicable to your subject line. Your email content must never embody any promise your business can't keep. Make your offer genuinely of value to your recipients.

4. Don't go too low.

If you inform your customers regarding discounts, minimal discounts are not that effective compared with substantial discounts. But never offer discounts that are lower than your profit. It will defeat the purpose of this email marketing effort.

5. Make it eventful.

It's not about contradicting the advice that you should keep an email short and sweet. This tip is on including seminars, conferences and other events in your email. Businesses that require training benefit much from this method. With these RSVP-requiring emails, repetition is important. Just make sure that an ample interval is considered before sending out a reminder email.

6. Post news.

Sending newsletters and postcards provides useful information for your subscribers. These are the best forms of reaching out to your customers or prospects. You should keep the information short, simple and direct to the point for this feat to be effective.

With these simple ways of going about your email marketing endeavor, your business will prosper in no time.

The Best Internet Advertising is Free Internet Advertising

Free internet advertising is one very important method for promoting your products and services to thousands of free classified ads.

Most of these free classified ads web sites give you the power to facilitate marketing with features such as classified ads submitter forms. Features like this give free Internet advertising an extremely fast way of getting your products or services on line. It is accessible 24/7 allowing you access anytime, it's very effective and efficient and most of it comes free. No downloads. No sign-up fees. No hidden charges. No annual or monthly fees. No sales fees. It is absolutely free.

Free internet advertising makes it easy for you to put free ads on several of the premier quality web sites whenever you want, for free. This kind of benefit you get from free internet advertising can only do, to say the least, miracles for your business. Most of these free internet advertising companies give you 3 slots to advertise any product or service for free.

Free internet advertising is the perfect way and best way to make your products or services known to the millions of prospective consumers in the Internet and make your web site start producing money. There is an enormous audience for free internet advertising that is present in the Internet, that the probability of anyone needing your services or wanting to buy your products is very high. There are free services out there that may suit your services, products and web site. Browse the internet for the best free internet advertising for assessment on their amenities and features how to advertise or join your web site for free internet advertising.

Most web sites promoting free internet advertising have features like classified ads submitter – where you can get a enormous exposure with instant results and expand your sales by large volumes over night, opt-in email lists – non spam bulk emailing program, guaranteed 100% legal. Opt-in email lists are created by people who have volunteered or 'opted-in' their email addresses to these lists. These lists are very effective for creating personalized email to prospective clients.

Free internet advertising provides a great technique for building traffic. People constantly search on online free internet advertising ads for specific services or products. Free internet advertising target clients inclined to buying a particular kind of product or service in mind.

And the best reason to advertise in free internet advertising is because it is absolutely free.

Free Internet Marketing Methods that will Save your Internet Business

Best things in life are free, as many would say. This especially holds true with efforts in advertising one's products or services. With free Internet marketing services, one can save a lot. Instead of shelling out for the marketing aspect of your product or services, that chunk of money could be put to other important elements of your business since many information websites now offer knowledge regarding Internet marketing services that comes with no price tag at all.

This is not to tell you that better focus on plain Internet marketing. It still will do your business a lot good if you mix traditional advertisement efforts such as traditional and new marketing media.

Here are few of the free methods that you could employ to make your products and services be in their most visible, thus saleable, form.

1. Promote your business through free search engine submission and optimization.

Submit your website to various search engines monthly. This will make many more people know that your website actually exists. Aiming for the top search engines will help a lot in this endeavor.

2. Improve your articles.

Remember that information on articles with good content as traffic-bringer of websites? This time it's about making these articles serve your website better by using keyword suggestion tools that are offered for free. Update your web site's content by regularly checking the standing of your keywords with the current market.

3. Acquire free content.

If you have no time to increase the SEO or search engine optimization-friendliness of your articles, you can look for free content from article directories. All you need to do is retain the resource box of those write-ups.

4. Avail of free comprehensive web traffic analyzers.

These are tools that you can make use of without costing you a cent. Your website's hits statistics will be produced by this kind of Internet marketing tool for your own analysis.

5. Learn to manipulate web design templates.

You don't have to be too techie-geeky to be able to design your web site. Oftentimes, web design templates or custom-made layouts are available for the Internet marketer to use.

6. Monitor your website's visibility.

Tools such as search engine position trackers may be used to see your website's standing.

These processes are very convenient to use as long as you keep in mind that you use and try to master their use for your own benefit. Just don't get obsessed with your achievements when you finally learn how to use them and incorporate them in your Internet marketing feat.

How to Acquire Free Web Site Promotion

You have finished making your own website. You have introduced your company and presented your products and services. You have added propositions and promos to catch your target audience's attention. You have achieved the dos and don'ts of building a company web site. But why isn't your website a major success?

Maybe you're not planning the key to the best promotion of your web site. Here are some guidelines on how to acquire free web site promotions for your company's success.

If you have started to promote your web site, keep it constant. If you promote your site with persistence, it will catch your audience's attention.

Be patient. Try each method in promotion until you acquire the best, free promotion there is. You have to accept trial and error for your web site to reach the top.

There are many ways for your web site to be seen. Here are some free web site promotions you could try until you find the most effective.

*Free promotions such as search engines and directories would give your web site the deserved traffic you always wanted. Make sure to check your web site's ranking to know whether or not this type of free promotion is right for you.

*Make a deal with other web sites on trading links which could help both web sites. Make sure to use words that could easily interest the audience.

*Find free classified ads that could boost the promotion of your web site. These ads could be seen by other people who you are not targeting for, but may as well be interested in your services.

*Free and low-cost internet banners are spread all through out the World Wide Web. Banners that pop-up at the top of a page or in a separate window would automatically catch your target audience's attention.

If your web site and its free promotion did not work even after accomplishing these methods, analyze your web site. Track down all visitors, advertisements, and transactions. Then locate errors in your web site. Upload new files to your web site continuously for audience to return for new products and services. Monitor your own web site if it's up in the market or down.

Then be ready to try the methods again and surely it will work.

It has always been said that the best things in life are free. Yes they are. And as soon as your free web site promotion proves to the audience its worth, then you'll believe it's true.

Three Traffic Tactics that won't Cost You a Cent

Are you constantly banging your head in frustration on not receiving all the internet traffic you would like to get to your web site? Are you tormented from information overload listening to all the latest free website traffic tactics and not being able to understand any of it? Are you dejected of people trying day and night to harassing you to max out your credit card and get loans for Google clicks, and in the process loose your credit score? Are you stupefied by the way your website just dropped out of the Google search results? Or are you just too broke and all you have to rely on is getting some free website traffic tactics?

You can employ website traffic tactics without spending dime. However, knowing how is the real deal. Here's the score:

1. Link it

Of all the effective website traffic tactics that can get you best results, linking to and from other websites is the one of the most widely-used method. Just make sure that the Internet business you are exchanging links with is relatively if not utterly related to your own business. And of course, don't overkill as this might ban you from search engines.

2. Meet Meta Tags

Another way of to acquire your desired traffic for your website is through having your Meta tags contain usually used keywords that target your business. Meta tags help search engines in describing your web page. If you're quite adept with the HTML aspect of your web pages, manipulating your meta tags would be a breeze.

3. Keyword-rich AND sensible content

Writing or acquiring articles that provide solid information regarding your business is one of the best ways. Making use of free keyword suggestion tools such as Overture will help you on which keyword or phrases to work on to better lead more traffic to your website. Making these write-ups very readable and genuinely informative will make you many repeat visitors to subsequently become repeat clients.

Submitting these articles to various article directory listings will provide more visibility for your business as long as you keep your resource box in tact to create for yourself numerous back links.

These methods, if employed properly, will not only make your web site popular but will make you achieve your most desirable result - higher conversion rate.

All About Internet Advertising Methods

People opt for internet advertising methods because practically half of the world's population knows HTML. If you have your own business, you have to decide on what internet advertising method works for you. Ask yourself what are you going to avail of: the expensive internet advertising methods or the cheap ones? Others will pipe in "expensive!" immediately, but they don't know cheap internet advertising method attracts great benefits as well.

Here's the lowdown and a comparative look on the cheap and expensive internet advertising methods:

The Expensive:

1. Pop-ups. Not only is this expensive, but also outright annoying that visitors close pop-up windows without even bothering to know what they're all about. This is an internet advertising method that you can do without.

Fly ads are derivatives of pop-ups which are also equally irking to the visitors.

2. 1. Pop-ups. Not only is this expensive, but also outright annoying that visitors close pop-up windows without even bothering to know what they're all about. This is an internet advertising method that you can do without.

Fly ads are derivatives of pop-ups which are also equally irking to the visitors.

2. Pod casts.

Broadcast is to TV as pod cast is to internet. It's one sophisticated internet advertising method that can somehow hamper your budget. But if you're thinking results, pod casting is worth the money.

3. Paying the search engines.

How does this one work? When someone types in a keyword related to your site, your URL is automatically included in the first page of the top results. Fixed payment for the search engine allows just that. Expensive, yes, but if we're talking about Google and Yahoo search engines here, then don't give it a second thought.

This is associated with another internet advertising method: the pay-per-click system.

The Cheap:

1. Blogging.

Go along the bandwagon and blog about your website. This is an internet advertising method that is popular as of the moment, so you never have to worry that this will never spur outcome. All you have to do is sign up for a blogging account, post and voila! You don't even need to pay!

2. Submit to not-so-big search engines.

This is cheap and dependable. If you submit your site to smaller search engines, you have bigger chances to get bigger results. Remember that the search engine giants can dwarf and overlook your site easily, so this internet advertising method might just be the right one for you.

3. Text links.

This is not just cheap...this is virtually free! Let someone text link your site and return the favor.

Cheap versus expensive, that's always the question that hounds on whenever we're trying to get something. In the field of internet advertising, just be wise enough to figure out what will suit your needs. Go for what you want as long as there are visible results.

Low cost advanced website traffic tactics for everyone

Advanced website traffic tactics might sound daunting, but if you make it low cost then you have nothing but a win-win situation. Employ low cost advanced website traffic tactics and you're in for a huge online success.

What are these low cost advanced website traffic tactics anyway? Surprise yourself by finding out that some of these tactics you can practice without having to spend a cent!

1. Write an article.

You write an article, mention your site, submit it to e-zines and garner traffic from curious visitors. It's as simple as that. Don't just stop at one website - post your site anywhere possible! Who knows how many hits this low cost advanced website traffic tactic will bring!

2. Exchange links.

Never underestimate the power of link exchange. This is a low cost advanced website traffic tactic that people tend to overlook. How to find out where to do the link exchange? Easy: type your website's keywords in a major search engine, visit each and every of the top results and ask for the link exchange.

3. Get involved in forums.

Look for forums highly related to your website and make your presence known. Make online friends and let them know about your website. This is an advanced website traffic tactic that advertises subtly but works effectively. Good thing about this is it doesn't cost you anything at all!

4. Advanced website traffic needs advanced tools.

The www world is rich with tools that churn out impressive results. Software to try out are those which take care of links and keywords. Once this is taken care of, the rest of this internet marketing job will be easy!

5. Power up with meta tags.

Meta tags are what search engines are looking for so it can include your site in the top results. Putting up meta tags in your HTML code is an advanced website traffic tactic that must not be missed! Low cost you ask? Oh yeah!

6. Direct to directories.

Keep submitting your site to directories like there's no tomorrow! Just take a look at your website and see if it's directory-worthy. Web directories don't waste their time on poorly-done websites.

7. Conduct a survey.

Visit a site similar to yours and announce that you have a survey they can answer. The site and yours reap results so no one's on the losing end here!

There are sites available that specialize in low cost advanced website traffic tactics. Search for them online and let your site rise to online popularity!

Low Cost Advertising and Scams on the Internet

"A business without a sign is a sign of no business". This is an advertising banner or quotation that can be seen in large billboards along the roads and on the side or top of buildings that is vacant. Television and radio would say, "This program would not be shown or be heard without advertisement". It is true since most of us are watching the free television channel and programs are produced by payments of advertisements.

Business owners understand how important an advertisement is. It is in this manner that they would tell to everybody that they are selling products and offering services. They would not have sales, which in turn give them profit, if people would not notice and buy their products and avail of their services.

However, it is not happy to note that there are people who would try to steal money from advertisers and business owners by offering cheap advertisement packages and not delivering the agreed service. Business owners and advertisers should be informed of this because they would become victims of a scam.

The scam here is when the advertiser paid for these different kinds of services but none or some of them are not really even performed. The main point to consider here is to whom is the advertiser transacting with. To avoid being ripped off doing a background check by knowing the following will help.

-past successful projects as evident on customers comments

-a good reputation that will be confirmed by his references, (people that he's had past transaction with and that are also reputable)

The pay-per-click ad campaign is when an advertiser would pay a certain agreed amount by the search engine developers every time a user clicks on that banner. This was a good idea before it was not touched by hackers who developed a certain program to automatically click on that banner which increases the amount to be paid by the advertiser. The next paying scheme was the "pay per action", which is harder to hack since the advertiser would only pay the search engine developers an agreed amount every time a sale would be done on that customer.

One thing is for sure, advertising in the Internet is not easy but it is fun, especially when one understands fully the power of the Internet. It is not a unidirectional means of advertising like the television or radio, but it is an interactive avenue for both the advertiser and the prospective clients.

Aggressive Internet Marketing Made Possible

Aggressive internet marketing means full-blown marketing and promotions that exceed any businessman's expectations. A business needs fierce internet marketing. No more, no less. But to make it low cost? Is that even possible? How can something so aggressive be affordable?

Luckily, you can avail of inexpensive aggressive internet marketing if you just look hard and good enough. Be keen and alert and know what's going on in the online industry. The following questions will help you discern if your chosen internet site to do the marketing fits the bill.

1. Does the company offer free website design?

Even if you know your HTML, it is still more advisable if a professional team does it for you. Some internet marketing sites offer free web design to make sure that your site's needs are met. It's a must that marketing is integrated to the web design.   If the company requires you to pay more than fifty bucks for the web design, then so much for straight-forward internet marketing! Look somewhere else!

2. How many keywords does your web site cater to?

Having too many keywords or key phrases to focus on will make your page ranking drop. Creating smaller web pages with content that emphasizes only a few keywords will serve Internet marketing endeavor better.

3. How search engine-compatible is your website?

Internet marketing is coined "aggressive" only if it is a hundred percent search engine-compatible. There are about 10 major search engines online and your site has to work accordingly with them. Find out if your internet marketing site is expert on search engine optimization.

4. Do you know your competitors?

Affordable aggressive internet marketing pushes your business forward by taking note of your competitors. Analysis and evaluation of the competition is mandatory to figure out your shortcomings and advantages over them. If this feature is excluded from your internet marketing plan, you're getting a mediocre deal.

5. How efficient is the monthly marketing plan?

Usually, you're asked to pay a monthly fee for the marketing plan. For a marketing plan to be efficient, it must zero in on the following things: webpage development, link exchanges, web content, updates and technical support. Of course, also included are the standard SEO, competition analysis and keyword density.

If you've procured the right answers for the previous questions, then you can finally say: "Now that's low cost aggressive internet marketing."

Affordable Advertising Agencies

Low cost internet advertising agencies are the ideal way and most recommended means to make your product or service known and for your web site to earn money. There is such a very huge range of affordable internet advertising agencies that are now found in the Net.

There are various Internet advertising agencies according to the kind of product or service they provide. Here is a list of a few of these kinds of online marketing agencies.

1. Web design agencies

These are focused on building web pages for a website. Many web developers are now offering affordable services if you just know how and where to find them.

2. Logo services

Production of web site logos is the main concern of these agencies. Hundreds of pre-designed logos could be purchased or even customized to complement your website better.

3. Copywriting Agencies

In adjunct to search engine optimization, these agencies provide quality content that targets the attention of the market you intend to tap. Looking for the best deals with copywriting services will be a cinch if you know where to look. If you prefer freelancers, they are often found with their own websites.

4. Search engine optimization companies

These companies analyze and modify websites in order to achieve the highest possible search engine ranking. They improve your website's design and content to better attract more traffic. Link building could also be employed by these e-marketing agencies to benefit your business. They are actually a combination of all the services mentioned above. Sometimes they also go by the name of Internet marketing consultancies or something of that sort.

5. Domain registration companies

Your business's name in the web is the business of these companies. Looking for the best amongst a wide array of these agencies is like looking for a needle in a haystack. But if you are determined enough to do your homework with these marketing services, results would be more than rewarding. Just make sure that you don't register with those whose only intention is to rip off those who can't afford the most reputable domain registration agencies.

These are just a few of the Internet advertising agencies that a web marketing newbie could turn to. Examining your needs first will better your chances in getting in touch with the cream of the crop of these Internet marketing agencies minus the hefty price tag.

Low Cost Internet Advertising Solution versus Conventional Advertising

Since the early 90's, the internet has become known as a medium for advertising. It has also been preferred by consumers and businessmen in public shopping and business dealings. Unlike any other media, like television, radio and print, internet advertising solutions with its low cost has become widely used.

Due to the considerable growth in figures of internet users and because of the inexpensive internet advertising solutions, it has more capability for multimedia subject matter. It could capture texts, images, video and audio. The advertisers could produce logos, moving banners, animated and 3d imagery. With these in hand, advertisers mix these forms to produce successful and low cost internet advertising solutions.

Not only does an affordable internet advertising solution serve as a communication station, it also assists in an effortless system for transaction and distribution. This is the only medium that could help people do business within a short period of time.

With just one click and a money-saving internet advertising solution, shoppers could get all the information they need by visiting any web site. The businessman could obtain the services he needs. The company is happy doing business with their clients. The clients are happy doing business in the comfort of their homes.

Unlike meeting in person, wherein time and money could be wasted, the low cost internet advertising solutions benefits the company in which the services and products are receiving sales. Plus, it also benefits the consumers who receive comfort and satisfaction guaranteed.

Inexpensive internet advertising solutions are able to lead other advertising medium because they were developed to be interactive. When a consumer reads and clicks on a web advertisement, it is easier and more convenient to respond or inquire with e-mail and business reply cards. Unlike other advertisings, low cost internet advertising solutions' ability to answer feed backs in real time enables the companies to reply, resolves complaints and answer inquiries.

Internet advertising solutions provide a low cost and effective resolution for attracting targeted, high quality customers. This low cost internet advertising solution also provides web site publishers with a prospect to generate advertising revenue from their unsold marketing inventory.

Conventional advertising could never be replaced. However, because of developments in the technology, people prefer their services online. With low cost internet advertising solutions present, the consumers, companies, advertisers and even the common people's lives have been given a deserving contentment.

Internet Marketing Strategies that Won't Hurt Your Savings Much

Your new business will benefit a lot from various Internet marketing methods. But you don't have to spend millions of dollars just to get some decent exposure for your company. There are ways to make your business be seen and felt without doing overkill with your advertisement expenses.

Make use of your online power - through Internet marketing. Here are simple methods that you may employ to boost the visibility of your business without shelling out more than what you can afford. However, these techniques need patience and some footwork to produce agreeable results.

Firstly, you need a website before you can make use of these low cost Internet marketing strategies. So go create one or hire a web developer. It will display your products and services. This will be used in employing the following Internet marketing techniques.

1. Affiliate Marketing

This is the process of recruiting a network of smaller websites known as affiliates to drive targeted traffic to a website. Ad copy and links will be provided by the advertisers. You will have to pay a certain percentage of the sales profit to your affiliates.

2. Links

One of your goals should be to attain a good ranking with search engines. One way to do it is through link building. This could be done through trading links to other businesses that are related with yours.

3. Newsletters

Sending out newsletters to your subscribers (those who signed up for your newsletters) will help greatly in establishing a good working relationship with your customers or prospective customers. It has to be short, sweet, consistent and written for a general audience.

4. E-mail Marketing

As one of the best cost-effective Internet marketing tools, it stays as a very important method of keeping your customers aware of your products and services. Just make sure to avoid spamming or soon enough you will have to close down you business due to complaints.

5. Articles

If you put quality content in the form of articles in your website along with your products and services, search engines will have to index your website. Getting you website indexed by popular search engines means more traffic for you.

6. Forums

Expand your Internet network is through joining forums that mainly discusses stuff regarding or related to your products and services. Actively posting responses or answers and asking relevant information will build your reputation as that forum's member and boost your company's visibility through your signature files. These signature files are those that go with your every post. Links to your website could be included in this signature.

Tool Talk: All about internet marketing tools

Who doesn't want inexpensive internet marketing tools? In this day and age when advertising your business online is the way to go, it's a must that you avail of internet marketing tools at the lowest cost possible. How can you avail of them? How can you make the most out of these low cost internet marketing tools?

These low cost internet marketing tools aim to better your website and promote them thoroughly. Read on to know more about them:

1. Software

There is software specializing in internet marketing. These programs are affordable internet marketing tools. They attract traffic, communicate your site to anyone online, harness and trim down your keywords, track your site visitors and create links to other sites. Of course, the phrase "low cost" emphasizes that you must not spend exorbitantly. Watch out for internet marketing tools that do nothing but suck your budget.

2. Website packages

Take note of low cost internet marketing tools that do the following: hosting and designing your site, getting your domain, offering technical help, configure and upload your files, campaigning for your traffic. These are available in website packages that you can avail of anytime. Choose a package caters to your site's needs.

3. Mailing lists

Notice that when you visit the Bulk Mail folder of your email, you read nothing but website promotions. That's email marketing? It boosts your business like no other. Don't worry about spamming. There's such a thing as "safe lists" that make your mails spam-free. This is so easy to obtain. Look for mailing lists for sale and let the fun of emailing begin.

4. Data Submitters

This is a money-saving internet marketing tool that works like magic. Have a data submitter of your own and amass tremendously huge hits!

5. E-books

Integrate an e-book in your site for people to download. At such a cheap price, you keep people clamoring for more and visiting your site in the process. That's one affordable internet marketing tool for you.

6. SEO tools

Internet marketing is not complete without the standard SEO tools. Search engines remain as the major powerhouse in marketing so never leave this part out. Generate traffic through this effective low cost internet marketing tool!

Here's a reminder: when you see the low cost internet marketing tool banners online, never get persuaded easily. Study the package deals; analyze the contents and benefits before deciding if you want one.

Determining Quality and Low Cost Pay per Click Internet Advertising Services

As Pay per click's name suggests, you only pay for actual click through to your web site. Inexpensive Pay per click internet advertising lists your web site according to your bid for a certain search keyword. Of course, Web sites which pay more are ranked higher.

Pay-per-click internet advertising can be a very reasonable cost compared to other manner of promotion on the Internet. You don't pay any amount until a visitor actually clicks on your listing and go to see your web site. The low cost pay per click internet advertising counts how many visitors click on your listing and takes the money out of an account you have set up with them.

You host the images to be used in your low cost pay per click internet advertising, so you can monitor and change the banner at anytime. Targeted advertising in pay for clicks will help increase the amount of customers you obtain at a controlled cost.

There are many low cost pay per click internet advertising solutions available in the internet. All you have to make sure is that the advertising solution guarantees your satisfaction and your web site's traffic.

In determining good quality and affordable pay per click internet advertising service, make sure to run very carefully planned and structured promotions in order to boost the targeted traffic to your web site and increase guest conversion rate.

Make sure that the pay per click internet services you applied for studies your business as well as your competitors. Plus, don't forget to give specific details regarding your target audience for your web site.

After the cheap pay per click internet advertising solution has finished studying and analyzing your business, research to produce the most appropriate keywords for your business. The pay per click internet advertising solution would then prepare an exclusive copy of the advertisement to be able to catch the attention of the would-be web site visitors.

For successful pay per click internet advertising, you and the solutions should identify appropriate landing pages. If needed, a number of changes are suggested to construct the perfect landing page which would work for an entry point to your website.

It is one great way to increase the visibility of your new web site. It is the fastest growing marketing tool there is today. Because of a wide range of companies servicing inexpensive pay per click internet advertising solutions, you must be careful to choose which company to trust. You should be able to research the service quality they are willing to offer.

Effective SEO Comes Cheap

Search engine optimization or SEO is the hottest way to drive targeted traffic to your website. Maximizing the benefits of a well optimized website will yield lots of earnings for the marketer. However, optimizing your site might cost you thousands of dollars if you are not skilled in this area.

But to tell you the truth, you can essentially get information on low cost SEO anywhere in the Internet. But only several really show you how to work out an affordable search engine optimization endeavor. And those few that really inform include this article.

1. Link exchanges

One cheap SEO method that can get you best results is through link exchanges or linking to and from other web sites. Depending on the websites that you would like to exchange links with, this tool could even cost you nothing at all. Contact the author or owner of the web site you want to have a link exchange with. You will be surprised with the eventual spiking up of your page ranking using this means of getting your website optimized.

2. Write or acquire key word rich articles

Writing truly informative and keyword-rich articles is one surefire way to make your Internet business more visible than ever. It's either you write your own articles or you get them from article directories that allow you to post these articles on your website as long as you keep the resource box or the author's byline in tact. Just don't stuff your articles with keywords that even idiots would get bore of reading them. The readability and freshness of your articles will still be the basis of whether your writers will keep on coming back to your website or not.

3. Catchy Domain Name

What better will make your target visitors remember your website but with a very easy-to-recall domain name. Something sweet and short will prove to be very invaluable. Registering your domain name is not for free. But creativity is.

4. Organize your site navigation

Providing easy steps in navigating your site is one way to make your visitors become at ease with your site. This, in turn, will improve the flow of traffic to your website.

Low cost SEO is always evolving like any other approach in information technology. There are many methods that can very well land you on the top ten rankings of Google or on any other search engines. Some may cost a lot but there are methods that can give you the same results at a low price or you can even do on your own such as those mentioned above.

Two Basic Parts of a Low Cost Web Site Promotion

Anybody could own a web site. Anybody could up sell their own products and services to their target audience. Anyone could try to promote their web site with a low cost. But there are not many web sites that have a truly successful web site with traffic all day through. What these individuals or companies lack is the most essential factor of success – a low cost web site promotion that really works.

If you have been trying to promote your own web site and you have received traffic every hour, my hands are down for you. But for those people who need assistance, who does not have the patience to promote their own product and services, and lacks knowledge to properly advertise themselves, here are some guidelines to help you achieve success with a low cost web site promotion.

Search Engine Submission and Ranking are the two basic parts to a low cost web site promotion. Both of the parts have the same effect on the market of the web site – for your products and services presented in your web site catches the people's attention.

The first inexpensive method of web site promotion is the search engine submission. This first part is the act filing information and submitting your web site to search engines. There are two types of Search engine submission – manual and automatic. For a low cost and effective web site promotion, automatic submission is ideal because after filling up the information, a software program would forward this information to other search engines.

The second money-saving web site promotion is ranking. This refers to the numerical position in which your web site appears on a search engine, based upon the web site's criteria. Some search engines rank the order in which your search results appear primarily by how many other web sites link to each page. The leading web sites on this order would eventually fulfill a low cost web site promotion.

Other types of inexpensive web site promotion you could use to boost up traffic on your web site are banner advertising, classified ads, text links and section sponsorship. Banner advertisements pop up above and below web pages, and sometimes in another window. Text links and section sponsorship may cost more, but these methods helps in promoting to your specified target audience. It wouldn't harm your web site to try these methods.

Always remember that the effects of your not so costly web site promotion hits are increasing significantly each day. Don't waste time; find an effective and affordable web site promotion of your choice today.

Effective SEO Comes Cheap

Search engine optimization or SEO is the hottest way to drive targeted traffic to your website. Maximizing the benefits of a well-SEO'ed website will yield lots of earnings for the marketer. However, SEO-ing your site might cost you thousands of dollars if you are such a newbie on this field.

But to tell you the truth, you can essentially get information on low cost SEO anywhere in the Internet. But only several really show you how to work out an affordable search engine optimization endeavor. And those few that really inform include this article.

1. Link exchanges

One cheap SEO method that can get you best results is through link exchanges or linking to and from other web sites. Depending on the websites that you would like to exchange links with, this tool could even cost you nothing at all. Contact the author or owner of the web site you want to have a link exchange with. You will be surprised with the eventual spiking up of your page ranking using this means of getting your website optimized.

2. Write or acquire key word rich articles

Writing truly informative and keyword-rich articles is one surefire way to make your Internet business more visible than ever. It's either you write your own articles or you get them from article directories that allow you to post these articles on your website as long as you keep the resource box or the author's byline in tact. Just don't stuff your articles with keywords that even idiots would get bore of reading them. The readability and freshness of your articles will still be the basis of whether your writers will keep on coming back to your website or not.

3. Catchy Domain Name

What better will make your target visitors remember your website but with a very easy-to-recall domain name. Something sweet and short will prove to be very invaluable. Registering your domain name is not for free. But creativity is.

4. Organize your site navigation

Providing easy steps in navigating your site is one way to make your visitors become at ease with your site. This, in turn, will improve the flow of traffic to your website.

Low cost SEO is always evolving like any other approach in information technology. There are many methods that can very well land you on the top ten rankings of Google or on any other search engines. Some may cost a lot but there are methods that can give you the same results at a low price or you can even do on your own such as those mentioned above.

"Pay-Per Click" Ad Campaign: Earn More by Spending Less"

What is "Pay-Per Click"? "Pay-Per Click", is an easy to understand advertising strategy. There are around 300 million searches at major search engines everyday. This causes 80% of internet traffic. Placing your websites on these search engines is very important in reaching as many potential customers as possible. But in order to be seen and clicked most frequently, your website should be viewed at the top most of the search list. Most people only reach up to the third page of a search engine so the lower your rank, the lesser the chance you will be clicked. In "Pay-Per Click" advertising, you pay to be always visible on the internet. You select keywords or key phrases about your website, and the highest bidder ranks the best. There is no upfront cost. You only pay after a visitor clicks your link. This is why it is called "Pay-Per Click".

Everyday millions of people around the world click on Pay-Per Click Advertising Campaign. With the booming internet industry and the ever growing online business, an ad of virtually anybody on the planet can be seen on the internet anywhere in the world.

The "Pay-Per Click" advertising campaign is the premier growth area in online marketing. Last year, an estimated $741.2 million was spent on "Pay-Per Click" advertising. The usual search engine optimization can take weeks or even months to produce results. "Pay-Per Click" advertising can attract customers at an instant. Why? Because, this cutting edge ad campaign can be placed on any website and can be viewed by potential online customers, anywhere, anytime and all the time. The only challenge is placing the ads on proper websites that will attract possible customers for a specific product or services.

"Pay-Per Click" advertising campaign attracts the right consumers at the shortest possible time. This is the most cost effective way of marketing products or services. You can also monitor the customers who visit your site, what they are looking for and what they are buying. With the right creativity on using the right search-phrases, we can direct the right people who are willing to do business with us.

"Pay-Per Click" advertising can easily be managed 24 hours per day and 7 days a week through the internet. This allows you improve the campaign strategy by effectively responding to the activities of both customers and competitors.

So what are you waiting for? "Pay-Per Click" now and let your business take the fast route to success.

Free Website Promotion...Why Not?

Can you ever avail of free website promotion? Is that even feasible?

Of course yes! Nowadays, your baby website can amass huge traffic in no time thanks to free website promotion.

How does this free website promotion go anyway? What are things to be done?

1. Enlist your website.

Look for the hottest Internet directories and enlist your site there. This is the easiest and most effective free website promotion tactic. Start with this step and the rest of the good things will follow.

Just don't forget to prep your website and make it all spruced up for a higher chance to get accepted in your directory of choice.

2. Know your forums.

One reason why forums are created is for free website promotion for everyone. Log in, post actively, let them know about your site in every post and you attract instant visitors right there.

3. Write a press release.

Release your writing prowess and start up a press release that advertises your site! This is a free website promotion tactic that you can do anytime. Type a brief paragraph or two and email it to your friends, colleagues, internet e-zines, newspapers and other media and massive traffic will come to you pronto!

4. Be friendly online.

Free website promotion means you need to be friendly to other webmasters. Why, you ask? So they can link you immediately! Establish contacts and never tire of link requests and exchanges.

5. Write an article.

Say, your website is about your travel agency. Write an article about the perks of traveling or the hottest travel spots in the world. On the concluding paragraph, mention your website in passing. This article works as an advertorial and doubles as a free website promotion approach.

6. Just let the whole world know about your site.

What is free website promotion without the word of mouth? Insert your website, its URL and features in daily conversations and let the good news spread from one mouth to another!

7. Make a banner ad.

Make a banner ad for your site and ask another webmaster to do the same for his site. Then swap!

8. Take up a free website promotion course online.

Yes, there are free website promotion tutorials. But don't you know that you can actually take a free website promotion course that can help you out further? Part of the free website promotion program is signing up for newsletters.

When you make a website, you need not pay anything to promote it. You just read it -- there is such a thing as free website promotion!

"Maximum Exposure on Low Cost Internet Ad"

(Make the most of a low cost Internet advertising method)

Advertising had long since been a major determinant of a business' success. This would include the presentation of the product / service to the consumers. What really matters is how it is presented to the target market to be able to capture it.

Whatever the package, the ad media also plays a great role in determining the success of the product or service awareness.

What may be its advantages over other proven medium like the best-selling TV ads?

Advantages

1. Low Cost

Eventhough the Internet ad might be viewed as "classy" or far-reaching, as compared to other medium, this is far cheaper than most. Internet Ad Packages are offered for as low as $29.99 for a one-month run-time period.

2. Capture market

Should your product / service aim to cater to the younger generation or the corporate-oriented ones, Internet ad would be best since they would always be "hooked-up" into the net surfing sites that might have a link to your very own. Result, a great number of "hits" on your site!

2. Hassle free

All you would ever really need is a PC (and some knowledge and bright ideas in forming your site) wherein you could open your site, search for the best Internet Ad package, and check / update the status of your ad. You may actually never have to leave your home to advertise!

3. Updated ads

Unlike the TV ads that need to be updated on a regular basis, Internet ads may run for quite some time without the need for change. If so, change in the site is very minimal and may be done easily at home.

Disadvantages

1. Scope

Limited market may be captured if one would solely use the Internet Ad for advertising. Although most people now are into the use of technology, i.e. surfing the Internet, still, majority of the average consumers still relies on the old form of advertising as a means of gathering information about certain products / service.

2. Additional cost

If one would enlist the help of another professional or establishment to produce the site for their product or service, this would entail additional costs on the part of the entrepreneur.

Given the stated list of advantages and disadvantages about low-coast Internet Ad, an entrepreneur may now weigh in its applicability to his / her product or service.

The aim of Internet ad is to offer the widest range or "Maximum Exposure" of the brand at the least possible cost. Now, does that not sound good or what?

www.ingramcontent.com/pod-product-compliance
Lightning Source LLC
Chambersburg PA
CBHW051701170526
45167CB00002B/496